CREDO

CREDO

BY

KARL BARTH

WITH A FOREWORD BY
ROBERT McAFEE BROWN

Wipf & Stock
PUBLISHERS
Eugene, Oregon

Wipf and Stock Publishers
199 W 8th Ave, Suite 3
Eugene, OR 97401

Credo
By Barth, Karl
Copyright©1962 Theologischer Verlag Zurich
ISBN: 1-59752-119-1
Publication date 3/10/2005
Previously published by Charles Scribner's Sons, 1962

1935!

TO THE MINISTERS

HANS ASMUSSEN

HERMANN HESSE

KARL IMMER

MARTIN NIEMÖLLER

HEINRICH VOGEL

IN MEMORY OF ALL WHO

STOOD

STAND

AND WILL STAND

FOREWORD

ROBERT McAFEE BROWN
*Professor of Religion in the Special Programs
in Humanities, Stanford University*

C AN a book originally published in 1935
fairly represent the author's point of view
over a quarter of a century later? Particularly can this be so when the author in question is
Karl Barth, a man who has gone through a long
and radical theological pilgrimage?

When one glances over the course of Barth's pilgrimage, one notes certain milestones along the
way, certain points at which the path shifted in
a new and decisively different direction. There is
the original *Epistle to the Romans* of 1919, wholly
re-written in 1922, replete with references to Kier-
kegaard, existentialism, the "totally other" and
"the infinitely qualitative distinction between God
and man." There is the *Christliche Dogmatik* of
1927, in which Barth set forth a whole theological
program to be elaborated in future volumes. This
venture was halted almost as soon as it was under-
way, for in 1931 appeared a decisive volume, a
work on Anselm, in which Barth re-thought the

ix

nature of the theological task in the light of the Anselmic *credo ut intelligam*. The result was that the *Christliche Dogmatik* was scrapped, and re-written with a new title, *Kirchliche Dogmatik (Church Dogmatics)*, the first volume appearing in 1932. From this point on, Barth has pursued a generally consistent course. As successive volumes of the *Church Dogmatics* have appeared (and at this moment there are twelve, with at least two more promised), the shift, if there has been one, has only been toward what one of Barth's critics refers to as a greater and greater "Christological concentration."

In other words, the main lines of Barth's theological position had been secured by 1932, three years before the appearance of *Credo*. The latter is not, therefore, a "transition" volume, of interest only to those who wish to trace stages in Barth's development. While Barth would certainly say some things differently today (retracting, no doubt, his words about Sacraments in the closing pages) it is little short of amazing, reading *Credo* retrospectively in the light of the full *Church Dogmatics*, how much of the latter is here *in nuce* in this small book. The dissatisfaction with "natural theology," the centrality of Christology, the sheer "givenness" of the gift of grace to the undeserving, the recognition that we cannot really see the enormity of sin until we have been captured by the vastness of grace, the Christian life as the life of gratitude in response to the greatness of what God has done, the glad certainty that in Christ sin and death have truly been conquered and that a new situation is therefore always before us—these and other themes that the *Church Dogmatics* spells out over hundreds of pages, confront us here in a paragraph, a page, a chapter, in such a way that we discover that for Barth the tasks of exegete and preacher, scholar and proclaimer, teacher and witness, are all combined in one vocation.

That there is particular urgency behind these lectures is made clear by the date. They were given when the shadow of Hitler had already fallen across Europe. Evil days were ahead. Right conviction was important as a basis for right action, and Barth felt, properly, that wrong conviction could lead to wrong action. Then as now, reflection upon an historic utterance of the faith was not an evasion of the present, but a means of arming one's self to live responsibly in the present.

The reader has the privilege of disagreeing with Barth. He no longer has the privilege of ignoring him.

TRANSLATOR'S PREFACE

THIS book is more simple and popular than some of Karl Barth's other works. It can be understood by, and it certainly has a message for, every member of the Church. Unfortunately the most difficult part of the book comes at the beginning. It is because I do not want the general reader to lay down the book after the first few pages, that I transgress the translator's rule neither to be seen nor heard, and write this note. I suggest to the general reader that, in his first reading of the book, he start with the Fifth Chapter. Perhaps Karl Barth would be shocked if he knew that I was making such a suggestion, and yet I am not so sure. For him faith begins with Jesus Christ. The reader who starts with the Fifth Chapter, therefore, not only misses some difficult hurdles, but he begins where faith begins.

Though I have used the words "simple" and "popular" I do not mean that CREDO will be found as easy to read as the newspaper leader that we skim at the breakfast table. But it is worth a little pains, for it is a statement, by the Church's greatest living thinker, of the faith of the

Church.   In twenty years Karl Barth has, in God's providence, changed the whole direction of the Church's thought.   Every part of the Church of Christ throughout the whole world is to-day wrestling with the questions raised by him.   But many who are discussing these questions and quoting Barth's name have the weirdest ideas as to what Barth stands for.   This book will show that he is neither the iconoclast nor the spinner of daring speculative theories that some people imagine him to be, but that he is before all else a "Doctor of the Holy Scriptures".   He has brought the Church back to the Word of God.   If people must have a label for his theology, let them call it, not the "Dialectic Theology," not the "Theology of Crisis," but the Theology of the Word

This note is for "the man in the pew," whom I want to encourage to read this book.   Ministers and other specialists in theology will need no encouragement, but, beginning at the beginning, will, I am sure, find challenge and inspiration in every word of it.

CONTENTS

CREDO

TABULA RERUM

xvii

I

CREDO

THE attempt to state and to answer the " chief problems of Dogmatics " is here to be undertaken " with reference to the Apostles' Creed ". It will not be our business to inquire into the *origin* of this text. What is in mind is that Credo which has been familiar since the eighth century; which, already known about the year 200 and pointing back to a still earlier period, succeeded in establishing itself, in the various forms of a Roman symbol, in the Christian West; which passed into the **Rituale Romanum** and was then recognised by the Churches of the Reformation also, as the fundamental confession of the common Christian faith. Nor does a *historical analysis* of this text come within our purview. We use it simply as a basis for theological investigations, in the course of which we shall necessarily have to understand and explain it not only in the light of its own time, but also in the light of the whole (and therefore also of the later) historical development.

The Credo is fitted to be the basis of a discussion of the chief problems of Dogmatics not only because it furnishes, as it were, a ground-plan of Dogmatics but above all because the meaning, aim and essence of *Dogmatics* and the meaning, aim and essence of the *Credo*, if they are not identical, yet stand in the closest connection. In this first lecture we attempt to refer from the *conception of Credo*, as it stands at the head of the symbol (at once as beginning and title) to the *conception* in which we are interested, that *of Dogmatics*.

1. Like the corresponding Greek πιστεύω, *Credo* at the head of the symbol means first of all quite simply the act of recognition—in the shape of definite cognitions won from God's revelation—of the reality of God in its bearing upon man. Faith therefore is a decision—the exclusion of unbelief in, the overcoming of opposition to, this reality, the affirmation of its existence and validity. *Man* believes. And therefore : man makes this decision, *credo*. But what gives faith its seriousness and power is not that man makes a decision, nor even the way in which he makes it, his feelings, the movement of his will, the existential emotion generated. On the contrary, faith lives by its *object*. It lives by the call to which it responds. It lives by that, because and in so far as that is the call of *God : credo in unum Deum . . . et in Jesum Christum . . . et in Spiritum sanctum*. The seriousness and the power of faith are the seriousness and power of the *truth*, which is identical with God Himself, and which the believer has heard and received in the form of definite truths, in the form of articles of faith. And even the *disclosure* of this truth is a free gift that positively comes to meet the believing man. It is God's own revelation. In believing, man obeys by his decision the decision of God.

All this holds for Dogmatics also. It, too, is human recognition of the reality of God as it is revealed. It, too, lives by the truth that comes to man—as obedience to a decision of God over which man has no power. It, too, is carried out concretely—in the affirmation of definite truths, and in this process the truth of God becomes concretely man's own. Dogmatics, too, is in its substance

2

an act of faith. But the *special characteristic* of Dogmatics is that it wants to *understand* and *explain* itself. Dogmatics endeavours to take what is first said to it in the revelation of God's reality, and to think it over again in human thoughts and to say it over again in human speech. To that end Dogmatics *unfolds* and *displays* those truths in which the truth of God concretely meets us. It articulates again the articles of faith ; it attempts to see them and to make them plain in their interconnection and context ; where necessary it inquires after new articles of faith, i.e. articles that have not up to now been known and acknowledged. In all this, it would like to make clear and intelligible the fact that in faith we are concerned with the austere, yet healing sovereignty of the truth and to what extent this is so. Dogmatics is the act of the Credo determined by the scientific method appropriate to it—*credo, ut intelligam.*

2. Credo at the head of the symbol does not signify the act of faith of a well-disposed or gifted or even an especially enlightened individual as such. The act of the Credo is the act of *confession.* But the subject of confession is the *Church* and therefore not the individual as such nor in virtue of any human or even divine mark of individuality, but the individual solely in virtue of his bearing the mark of membership of the Church. When God's reality, as it affects man, is recognised by the Church in the form of definite cognitions won from God's revelation, then there comes into existence in this *eo ipso* public and responsible recognition a confession, a symbol, a dogma, a catechism ; then there come into existence articles of faith. When the individual says in the sense of the symbol, *credo,* he does not do that as an individual, but he *confesses,* and that means—he includes himself

3

in the *public* and *responsible* recognition made by the *Church*.

Dogmatics belongs entirely to the same sphere. It is indeed not itself confession ; but it is *allied with* it as the action of definite individual members of the confessing Church ; it is the elucidation of the current confession and the preparation of a new one. Because the Church must again and again understand its Confession anew and because it is again and again confronted with the necessity of confessing anew, it requires Dogmatics alongside of the Confession. There is no other justification for Dogmatics. An individual can be its subject only as commissioned " teacher of the Church," i.e. as teacher *in* the Church *from* the Church *for* the Church, not as savant, but as one who has a vocation to teach. The private character of the professor of Theology, his views and insights as such are matters of no interest. And the same is to be said of his hearers and readers as the future preachers. Lecturing on and study of Dogmatics are a *public* and *responsible* action inasmuch as only the Church —in Dogmatics just in the same way as in the Confession —can seriously speak and seriously hear.

3. The problem of the Credo as the Church Confession arises in the problem of the Church's *proclamation*. The good news of the reality of God as it affects man is entrusted to the Church. That is, entrusted to its *faith*. This, however, means among other things—entrusted to the *work* of its faith which is from the beginning tentative and fallible, entrusted to the human, the all too human, understanding and misunderstanding of the divine judgment, entrusted to the conflict and contradiction of human opinions and convictions. What becomes of the *purity* of that which has been entrusted to the hands of the

4

pardoned, who always were and will be nothing else than pardoned sinners ? The answer can be, and indeed must be : even in impure hands God can and God will keep it pure. But that does not exonerate us from concern for the purity of our hands or from searching after the *true* and *proper* proclamation. From this concern and this searching springs the Church's Confession. Confession is always the result of an effort motivated by this concern and searching, is always an attempt to protect divine truth from human error and to place it on the candle-stick. Confession is always concrete, historical decision, a *battle action* of the *Church*, which thinks that it hears, in various convictions and doctrines cropping up within its pale, the voice of unbelief, false belief or superstition, and feels compelled, along with the " Yes " of faith, to oppose to it the necessary " No " : for the purpose of purifying the human hands in face of the purity of the message entrusted to them in order that its proclamation may be a proper proclamation.

It is in this connection that Dogmatics gets its meaning and its task. It is no idle intellectual game. Nor is it research for research's sake. In explaining the Confession and preparing a new confession it performs that watch-man's office that is indispensable for the Church's pro-clamation. In face of the errors of the time it enters the breach where the old confession is no more regarded or no more understood and a new confession is not yet in existence. Certainly it cannot speak with the authority of the Church's Confession, but instead of that it can, as living science, act with greater mobility and adapta-bility in relation to the situation of the moment, with greater accuracy and point in the particular investiga-tion. Certainly like the Church's proclamation itself it

5

can deteriorate and run wild. It can very well be that, with regard to the Confession with which it is allied, it strays and leads astray. It can actually be that, instead of calling to order, Dogmatics has to be called to order and corrected by the Church's proclamation that has kept to better ways. Dogmatics is no more able than the Confession to be a mechanically effective safeguard of the good news in the Church. Yet a Church that is conscious of its responsibility towards what has been entrusted to it will always be mindful of these safeguards. What men do in Church can from beginning to end of the line be nothing else than *service*. He who acts in it is the Lord, He Himself and He alone. But just as along the whole line of Church service the function of the Confession is necessary, so also this function is necessary : the scientific examination of the Church's proclamation with regard to its genuineness. The existence of Dogmatics is the Church's admission that in its service it has cause to be humble, circumspect and careful.

4. But the Credo does not spring from any concern or questioning of the Church, acting on its own, in regard to the genuineness of its proclamation. Not arbitrarily does faith part company in the Credo with anything that it thinks faith should not hold ; not in any haphazard way does it say " Yes " here and " No " there. When the Confession makes its decisions it does not measure with the yard-stick of the ideas of truth, God, revelation and the like that happen to be current at the time, to-day this, to-morrow that, now under this prevailing point of view, now again under another. If it did that, it could not really itself be described and understood as an act of recognition, nor could it on its side make any claim to recognition. The value of the Confession lies in the fact

that when it was being formed the Church, in face of the ideas of the time, inquired into the decision of *Holy Scripture*, and in the Confession did not simply express its faith as such, but what in its faith it thought it heard as the judgment of the *Holy Scripture* in points of Church proclamation that had become doubtful. In the Credo the Church bows before that God Whom we did not seek and find—Who rather has sought and found us.

Now it is just from this that the worth of *Dogmatics* also derives. It is preceded by *Exegesis* as primary theological discipline. That means that *Dogmatics* does not carry its *norm* in itself, as also it does not have its *purpose* in itself, but is reminded by the discipline of Practical Theology that follows on after it, of its task within the whole sphere of the Church's service. The expert in Dogmatics is not the judge of Church proclamation. Only if he put more reliance on his philosophy or philosophy of religion than is permissible could he be willing to act as judge. His function is to point the Church's proclamation in its whole range to the *real* judge. The real judge is the prophetic and apostolic witness to revelation, as that witness speaks through the Holy Spirit to our spirit. Every dogmatic effort to elucidate the cognitions already expressed in the Credo, and every dogmatic stirring of cognitions that are waiting to be expressed in a future Credo can, in their true substance, exist only in the confrontation of the propositions on occasion uttered in the Church with this judge. What Dogmatics has to exhibit with the utmost conscientiousness is the discussion that is inevitable when these two meet. No limitation or modification of this rule is involved when we add that any arbitrary appeal on the part of Dogmatics to the very Bible itself is forbidden

7

by the fact that it is itself confession-bound, i.e. that it remembers its definite place in the Church, and therefore brings to the Confessions, in which the Church has already definitely expressed its understanding of the Bible, that respect which children owe by God's command to the word of their human fathers.

5. The Credo finally shows the Church engaged in *missionary* work, directed towards the world which is not yet gathered into the Church, facing it with responsibility and appeal. How else is it to explain and defend itself, how else recruit and invite, link up and try to gain ground with its message than by *confessing* its *faith*, as far as possible in its fullness and yet in the shortest words, as free as possible from everything accidental, as far as possible purified from every ambiguity, as definite as it is possible for faith to be, i.e. in its relation to the object from which it derives its life ? Even the material content of the Church's proclamation will always have to be the Credo. Among all human factors only the fact of *faith* is able to summon to faith. In the Credo the Church attempts to place this *fact* on the map.

In Dogmatics, also, it is able to do and aims at doing nothing else. What is here added is the *explanation* of the Credo. It gives to the fact of faith a breadth, a distinctness and perspicuity in which the Credo as such is lacking. Dogmatics is the Credo speaking here and to-day, speaking exactly according to the needs of the moment. Be it understood : the missionary and apologetic power can even here be nothing else than faith, or the testimony to its object, or its object itself. Dogmatics has no means of throwing other bridges between Church and world than that of the Confession. But its very attempt to exhibit the Confession as, on its Scripture basis, self-consistent and comprehensible, is able to give to the Confession a peculiar language, which, with its peculiar dangers, yet also has its peculiar promise. And let it not be imagined that it is only perhaps in scientifically employed or oriented circles that many are looking for just this language, the language of the dogmatically rigorous and detailed confession.

6. What has been said would not be complete if finally we did not also remember the *limits* of the Credo and so also of Dogmatics. The life of the Church is not exhausted by its confessing its faith. The Credo as such and Dogmatics as such can by no means guarantee that proper proclamation with which they are connected. They are only a proposal and attempt in that direction. And even proper proclamation, secured not only on the human side by the Credo and Dogmatics, but really and decisively secured by God's grace, has in the life of the Church three inevitable *frontiers :*

The first is the *Sacrament,* through which the Church is reminded that all its words, even those blessed and authenticated by God's Word and Spirit, can do no more than aim at that event itself, in which God in His reality has to do with man. Just these visible signs of Baptism and Holy Communion have manifestly, in the life of the Church, the important function of making visible the bounds between what can be said, understood and to that extent comprehended of God by man—and the incomprehensibility in which God in Himself and for us really *is* Who He is.

The second frontier of the Credo and Dogmatics is very simply our actual *human life,* in its weakness and strength, in its confusion and clarity, in its sinfulness and hope, that human life of which all the Church's words certainly *do* speak, without as words reaching and touching it, even where God Himself bears His witness to them. Much criticism and depreciation of Dogma and Dogmatics would remain unuttered if it were only clearly understood that human words as such *must* indeed serve the end, but can do no more than *serve* the end that our actual life be placed under God's judgment and grace.

The third frontier is the frontier which separates *eternity* from time, the coming Kingdom of God from the present age, the *eschaton* from the *hic et nunc*. Credo and Dogmatics without doubt stand together under the word of Paul (i Cor. xiii. 8 f.) according to which our gnosis and our prophecy are in like manner in part and will be done away, childish speech that will have to be put away when manhood is reached, a seeing in the dark mirror, not yet a seeing face to face. Meaning, essence and task of the Credo and of Dogmatics are based on conditions which, when God is all in all, will undoubtedly no longer prevail.

The existence of these three frontiers or limits might well be named at the outset *the* chief problem of Dogmatics. In any case we must never for a moment forget them. All that was said at the beginning holds good within these limits. And rightly understood, the very existence of these limits will no doubt give to what has been said a peculiar importance. Where you have limit, there you have also relationship and contact. Credo and Dogmatics stand facing the Sacrament, facing human life, facing the coming age, *distinguished* from them, but *facing* them ! Perhaps in the way in which Moses in his death faced the land of Canaan, perhaps as John the Baptist faced Jesus Christ. Could anything more significant be said of them than this, their limitation ?

II

IN DEUM

IF the symbol begins with the decisive word, " I
believe *in God,*" and if it is permissible for us to
characterise this its first word as also the cardinal proposition of Dogmatics, then we must go on to establish
the following : The relationship between this "in God"
and what follows in the three parts of the symbol with
regard to Father, Son and Holy Spirit cannot and must
not in any circumstances be understood in the sense that
this " in God " signifies, as it were, the specification of
a general concept of known content which then receives
in the three parts of the symbol its special historical
ingredients, namely, the Christian filling out and elabora-
tion. " God " in the meaning of the symbol—of the
symbol which aims at giving again the testimony of the
prophets and apostles—" God " is not a magnitude, with
which the believer is already acquainted before he is a
believer, so that as believer he merely experiences an
improvement and enrichment of knowledge that he already
had. When Paul says (Rom. i. 19) that what can be
known of God (τὸ γνωστὸν τοῦ θεοῦ, *cognoscibile Dei*) is
manifest to them, for God manifested it unto them, the
whole context as well as the immediately preceding
statement (Rom. i. 18) shows that Paul sees the truth
about God " held down " among men, made ineffective,
unfruitful. What comes of it in their hands is idolatry.
And with Paul, as with all the prophets and apostles,

idolatry is not a preparatory form of the service of the true God, but its perversion into the very opposite, to which therefore they, with their witness to God, do *not* attach but oppose their witness. The single point of contact—one that, it seems to me, is employed very ironically—is reckoned by Paul the altar of the *un*known God (Acts xvii. 23). The word " God " in the symbol, therefore, must not mislead us into first giving consideration to the nature and the attributes of a being which, on the basis of our most comprehensive experiences and deepest reflection, we think we have discovered as that which this name may and must fit, in order thereupon, under the guidance of the historical statements of the symbol, to ascribe to the subject so conceived this and that definite predicate, behaviour and act. On the contrary, we have to begin with the admission that of ourselves we do *not* know what we say when we say " God," i.e. that all that we think we know when we say " God " does not reach and comprehend Him Who is called " God " in the symbol, but always one of our self-conceived and self-made idols, whether it is " spirit " or " nature," " fate " or " idea " that we really have in view. But even this admission, of course, cannot carry the meaning that in it we are proclaiming a discovery of our own. The " unknown God " of the Athenians, the God of the agnostics was, to Paul's view, an idol like all the rest. Only God's revelation, not our reason despairing of itself, can carry us over from God's incomprehensibility.

In telling us that God is Father, Son and Holy Spirit, the symbol, which speaks of God on the basis and in the sense of the prophetic-apostolic witness, expresses absolutely for the first and only time *Who* God is and *What* God is. God is God precisely and only in that being and action which are here, in a new and peculiar way, designated as those of the Father, the Son and the Holy Spirit. Only in this reality of His that bears on us is God God. All our preconceived representations and ideas of what from our own consciousness we think we are compelled to take for " God," have, when we confess, " I believe in God," not indeed to disappear—for they cannot do that ; that would mean that we should have to remain speechless—but to give way before the utterance of revelation, to subordinate themselves to it completely and absolutely. They have to receive from it not only a new content, but also a new form. They are not only improved and enriched, but they are turned upside down. They are appointed to a service for which they have in themselves no capacity, for which they are absolutely unfitted and unequal, so that even now, namely, in the Confession of the Christian faith, we shall have to keep admitting that God remains incomprehensible to us, i.e. that we cannot comprehend to what extent we are now really speaking of God on the basis of God's revelation, in using the language of our preconceived representations and ideas. It is not because we have already sought Him that we find Him in faith, but, it is because He has first of all found us that we seek Him—now really *Him*— in faith. Truly and only as Father, Son and Holy Spirit, as Who He has revealed and will reveal Himself to us, is God God—He is not also God in addition in the thoughts of our hearts and in the works of our hands. It is just the man who has received God's revelation, who will ascribe God's being present as God to him, entirely to His revelation and not at all to himself, entirely to grace and not at all to nature.

We shall return in other places to the three names and

modes of existence of God as the Father, the Son and the Holy Spirit in their difference and unity, and in this Lecture dwell upon the formal—but yet only apparently formal—fact that " God " in the symbol is absolutely and exclusively He Who exists under these three names in these three modes of being, that is to say, absolutely and exclusively *God in His revelation.* If that is so, what does it mean to " believe in God " ? Who and What then is God ? Several answers are to be given to these questions, answers that will thereafter have to accompany us, warning us and directing us, on our whole way through the chief problems of Dogmatics.

1. He who believes in God in the sense of the symbol has the ground of a general faith in God (all of us as men always start out from that with its varied possibilities) taken away from under his feet in so far as he sees himself, in his confidence that man could of himself believe in God, confuted by God's revelation. The very fact of God's revelation signifies : Man cannot of himself really believe in God. It is because man cannot do that that God reveals Himself. What man of himself can believe in are gods who are not really God. When his confidence in his ability really to believe in God of himself goes to pieces, then the gods *fall*, in whom he really *can* believe. In the collapse of this confidence they are unmasked as gods who are not really God. But God is God in that we can *know* Him only on the basis of His revelation, not of ourselves, but only in opposition to ourselves, can believe in Him only by our becoming a miracle to ourselves. These are the indicatives that explain the imperative of the First Commandment : Thou shalt have no other gods before me ! The grace of revelation compels the dethronement of the other gods by,

first of all, forcing us ourselves down into the dust. He who believes lives by grace. He who lives by grace knows that he is forbidden to snatch at deity. He who knows that can indeed know the gods of the human heart, but he can no longer regard them as gods alongside of God. " I believe in God " therefore means : I believe in the one, the incomparable, the *only* God. The uniqueness of God is not a religious postulate nor a philosophic idea, but something that corresponds exactly to the uniqueness of God's revelation.

2. He who believes in God in the sense of the symbol has from God's revelation absolutely immovable ground under his feet when he thinks of God, reckons with God, speaks of God, points to God, abides by the name of God, and proclaims this name to others. He certainly does not believe in a God whom he has chosen for himself. Still less does he believe in the wisdom and power of his choice. He does not believe in his faith and consequently does not believe in himself. Therefore he cannot deal with God in the way in which we continually deal with our own ideas, hypotheses, convictions and opinions. They seem to us more or less certain. We can alter them and interchange them amongst themselves. We can drop them, take them up again and again drop them. They are the region of questioning, of doubt, of uncertainty, of dialectic. To this region God does *not* belong. In such a way one cannot deal with Him. Even the believer knows this region and lives in it. The believer, yes, only the believer, knows the despair that has the last word in this region. But the believer knows, beyond that, Him Who has chosen him, the man living in the midst of this sphere, and Who holds him over the abyss, all without his co-operation. This choosing and being chosen have

no part in the dialectic of our choice. Grace is superior to
nature and to all combinations of nature and grace, in
that it makes the believer certain of what he is about,
certain amid a thousand errors, weaknesses and vanities
into which even he may fall, certain in the greatest uncertainty, but also certain *in the teeth of* all uncertainty.
Faith in God, which is faith in God in His revelation and
nothing else, has something of the specific gravity of the
freedom, unchangeableness and *self-sufficiency* of God Himself. Not in the theoretical ascent from the finite to the
infinite do we recognise these attributes of God, but in the
proof of faith in God. They are counterparts of divine
self-revelation.

3. He who believes in God in the sense of the symbol is,
in the face of God, utterfully *thankful*. Not in himself, but
in God's revelation is the source of his having God, the
source of all that he has in God, of his believing in Him,
knowing and confessing Him. To him who, where God
is concerned, can only receive, not take, God's presence is
eo ipso a reconciling presence that creates communion
between God and man. The *law* that is imposed on him
by the presence of God, whether it drives him to repentance or detains him where he received forgiveness, that
also is grace. As grace also the *wrath* and the *judgment*
of God meet him although and indeed because he knows
that this wrath kills and this judgment is eternal. Grace
would mean to him—and this is not saying too much—
God's presence, even in the midst of *Hell*, if it were not
that faith would burst hell, conquer it and turn it into its
opposite. In proportion as man would like in face of God
to take to himself this and that, earn them, appropriate
them by his own power—in the same proportion he could
not be thankful, in the same proportion God's presence

would meet him as something else than grace, the law would necessarily offend and terrify him, and there would be no escape from God's wrath, from judgment and hell. How vitally important it is that with the symbol we understand by " God "—" God in His revelation" might be made particularly clear at this point. To believe in God may and must—if we are content to understand God in the sense of the symbol—mean : to believe in God's *kindness*. This is not that fictitious value, the *summum bonum*, not that maximum of what we consider good. It is that which, apart from all human opinions about good and evil, constrains the believer to thankfulness. Recognisable by faith as divine truth, it also is the counterpart to the action of God in His revelation.

4. He who believes in God in the sense of the symbol stands under God's *commands*. That he resists them, that he keeps transgressing them, that he fails to give honour to God and that he cannot stand his ground before Him, that also is true. But it is still truer that he *stands* under God's commands, that in his total foolishness and wickedness he is claimed by God, God's prisoner, that he must again and again make a fresh start with the commands of God, and return to them. True, he has no starting-points and no aims in which he could independently, i.e. of himself, know God's will. He could see in that only an arbitrary breaking loose into a freedom which does not become him. The freedom that becomes him is freedom from all other bonds. Believing in God, he is directed to God's word, *only* to God's word. Out of this bond he cannot completely escape either to please himself or others. It continually judges him, but it also holds him. Just because it is imposed on him without and indeed against his choice and volition, it is also comforting

17

to him. In placing him in the ultimate responsibility, it takes from him the ultimate responsibility for his life, it is geniune guidance. To believe in God means to believe in God's *holiness*. Even God's holiness is not a truth that can be ascertained as such by an observer. A merely observable divine holiness would most certainly be no more and nothing better than the ideal of an ethical world-view. God's holiness is apprehended in the fight of faith, in the sanctification of the believer through God's revelation. Being counterpart to what God does, faith apprehends that God is holy.

We have given several answers to the question, Who and What God is for him who believes in God in the sense of the symbol, who therefore believes absolutely and exclusively in God in His revelation. They were, if you will, formal answers, because we have not yet entered upon the great theme of the symbol itself, " God in His revelation," but have so to speak only touched it from outside from the point of view of its exclusiveness in relation to that theme that is very remote from the symbol, the theme " God in general ". But what is the meaning here of " formal " and " material," " outside " and " inside " ? In referring to the exclusiveness of this theme we have perhaps already caught a glimpse of the theme itself : the reality of God that has to do with man, the majesty of that God Who is Father, Son and Holy Ghost and Who cannot yield His honour to another. The indicative in the first commandment is indeed of a certainty no merely formal statement !

III

PATREM OMNIPOTENTEM

"**F**ATHER" and "Almighty" : these two first designations of God—each singly and the two in their interconnection—lead us at once into the fullness, into the light, and also into the darkness of the prophetic-apostolic testimony to revelation which is summarised in the symbol.

In the sense of the symbol and in line with what was worked out in the last Lecture towards an understanding of the Christian conception of God, we shall have immediately to make it clear to ourselves that the conception "Almighty" receives its light from the conception "Father" and not vice versa. And that, although it is undoubtedly God's revelation, and therefore an act of *divine* omnipotence through which God makes Himself known to man as Father ; although we undoubtedly know God the Father in the exhibition of His omnipotence. But an *act*, and that an act of *divine* omnipotence is the revelation of God's Fatherhood. God's omnipotence is not some power that we might be inclined to regard as omnipotence. It is the power of the Father that does not make itself known to us as omnipotence *in abstracto* but only as the omnipotence of the Father, and that means—in the Father's revealing Himself to us. This first article of the Creed and, in particular, these initial constituents are in no respect a playground for Natural Theology. It is not as if we already of ourselves knew what " omnipotence " is, in order then to have to learn from revelation only this in addition—that *God* is the Almighty and that the name and character of " Father " fit him. On the contrary, the revelation of God the Father is as such also the revelation of His omnipotence, and it is from this revelation that we have first of all to learn what real omnipotence is.

But according to the passages in Scripture where the conception " Father " gets its most pregnant meaning, the revelation of God the Father is the revelation of God in His Son Jesus Christ through the Holy Spirit. Scripture explicitly calls it the *sole* revelation of the Father. Therefore it is exclusively in this place that we shall have to seek to understand decisively and finally the conception " Father ". Let us start, however, from the fact that the revelation of the Almighty God and therefore of what in the sense of the symbol is called " omnipotence " is identical with the revelation of the Father of Jesus Christ through the Spirit, it being here that we have to learn what real " omnipotence " is.

With these words, " revelation of God the Father," we at once push into the sphere of faith's deepest mysteries. These words, " revelation of God the Father," contain a remarkable contradiction, so far as God as Father is just *not* manifest to us in revelation itself, or is manifest only as the God Who remains *hidden* from us even in His revelation and just there, Who, in disclosing Himself, conceals Himself, Who, in coming near to us, remains *far* from us, Who, in being kind to us, remains *holy*. " No man hath seen God at any time " (John i. 18). " He dwelleth in a light which no man can approach unto " (1 Tim. vi. 16). That, according to the Scriptures, is God the Father. God wants a faith in Himself as Father that expresses

itself in obedience, i.e. He wants to be known under the
condition that His hiddenness is recognised, to be known
in the act of His revelation, which means—in His *Son*
through the *Holy Spirit*. God's revelation in His Son
through the Spirit is a revelation which, far from exclud-
ing, includes within itself a *remaining* hidden, indeed a
profoundest *becoming* hidden on the part of God. God's
revelation in His Son, so far as we understand by that
concretely the—to us quite comprehensible—human
existence of Jesus Christ, is, as the second article of the
Creed will show us just as strikingly as is in keeping with
the New Testament, a way into the *darkness* of God ; it
is the way of Jesus to Golgotha. If as such it is a way
into the light of God, and is therefore really God's *revelation*, then that is because this Jesus on " the third day
rose again from the dead, He ascended into heaven, and
sitteth on the right hand of God ". But that is said of
Jesus the Crucified. Actually the hidden God here becomes manifest ; we are here led right to the limit of what
we can conceive in order that *here* (here, where Jesus
Himself cries : " My God, My God, why hast Thou forsaken me ? ") we may catch the words, " Behold, your
God ! " God the Father, as Father of Jesus Christ, is He
Who leads His Son into hell and out again. And in so far
as He, as Father of Jesus Christ, gives Himself through
the Holy Spirit to be known as *our* Father, we learn that
we can follow Christ only by taking up our Cross, that our
Baptism in His name is Baptism into His death and that
we must die with Him in order to live with Him (Rom.
vi. 3 f.), that our life, as the life of all His own, is a life
that is hid with Him in God (Col. iii. 3). Here, too, we
are led right to the frontier where our appropriate attitude can only be an obedience that marches out into the

darkness and a faith that steps out of the darkness into the light. Not more and not less than *the Lord over life and death* becomes manifest to us in the revelation of the Father through the Son in the Holy Spirit. This Lord over life and death is God the *Father*.

And it is just His lordship over life and death that is the *omnipotence* of God the Father. This is as different from the idea of an infinite potentiality as our real life is from one of our dreams. For infinite potentiality in itself and as idea is an empty conception under which no one has ever yet seriously imagined anything, because it simply cannot be done. But the omnipotence of the Father, revealed in the revelation of His Son through the Holy Spirit, is (in the obedience and faith given to this revelation) a reality which can be recognised as the totality of all known and conceivable and unknown possibilities. For the Lord over life and death with Whom we have here to do, is as such the Lord of our existence, i.e. He to Whom our life and with it our death has become bound, He Who at the utmost limit of all our possibilities commands us : Halt ! and at the very same place and instant : Forward ! to Whom therefore we effectively *belong*, i.e. in extremest fear and in greatest hope. That is " omnipotence " in a serious sense of the word. For the " all " (*omni*potence) in a serious sense means : the circle that is described by this claim of God to our life and to our death. And in a serious sense " power over all " means : the claim that thereby meets us, our being in subjection to this claim. All other " omnipotence " would not be real omnipotence. Only the claim of the Lord over life and death has real omnipotence. This real omnipotence becomes manifest to us in what the Scriptures call the " revelation of the Father ". This is the omnipotence of the divine decision legitimately made over us and recognised as such by us : this is infinite potentiality, because it is reality illimitably and unconditionally, because all possibilities, those known and those hidden, have in it their standard, their ground, their boundary and their definition, because we are really surrounded by it on all sides, sustained by it in every way, because along with our existence it rules also our world, rules it indeed completely. " Are not two sparrows sold for a farthing ? And one of them shall not fall on the ground without your Father. But the very hairs of your head are all numbered " (Matt. x. 29 f.). Once more, it is the revelation of the Father through the Son in the Holy Spirit which reveals to us this, the *real* omnipotence.

Now in this revelation of omnipotence, that is to say, in giving us His Son and the Holy Spirit for the knowing of His Son, God shows Himself as the *Father.* The act of omnipotence of the Lord over life and death in the revelation through the Son in the Spirit shows not only His omnipotence, but shows it as paternal ; it shows God's Fatherhood. It demonstrates and this demonstration is the truth that God *is* Father, not only and not first of all as *our* Father, but already in Himself *eternal* Father and precisely as such, *our* Father. So it is not the case that God only became Father, in relation to our existence and our world, by revealing Himself to us in the Son through the Spirit. Therefore it must not be said that the name " Father " for God is a transference to God, figurative and not to be taken literally, of a human creaturely relationship, whereas God's essential being as God *per se* is not touched nor characterised by this name, nay, He is infinitely above being Father to us, indeed is something different altogether. But what is figurative and not literal is that which we characterise and imagine we know as fatherhood in our human creaturely sphere. Figurative and not literal is even the Fatherhood of God in relation to our existence and world, as we recognise it in the revelation of His omnipotence as truth. We recognise it as *truth* and within the human creaturely sphere we speak of fatherhood in *truth*, because God *is* in truth Father : already beforehand, in eternity— which means even apart from our existence and world. He is the *eternal* Father, He is that in Himself. It is as such that He is then Father for *us* and reveals Himself to us and is the incomparable prototype of *all* human creaturely fatherhood : " from whom every fatherhood (πᾶσα πατριά) in heaven and earth is named " (Eph. iii. 15).

The statement that God is Father in truth, because from eternity to eternity, is, however, identical with the statement that, in revealing to us the Father, Jesus Christ is God's Son in the same strict sense, therefore, from eternity to eternity—and the Spirit, through Whom we know the Son and in the Son the Father, again in the same strict sense, therefore, from eternity to eternity is Holy Spirit, God Himself. That is to say, Scripture does not distinguish between a divine content, origin and object, and a non-divine or less divine shape or form of revelation. But where God in His omnipotence meets man in time and where man in time knows and acknowledges God's omnipotence, there in this double event Scripture sees God Himself in the arena no less than in the subject of this event itself. It is also this divine Subject Himself with Whom we have to do in the double event of revelation, that is, the objective and subjective event as such. God's revelation of omnipotence is, according to Scripture, a self-contained circle of divine

presence and divine action.   That exclusiveness belongs
to it for this reason : If the appearance of Jesus Christ
were to be regarded as some sort of theophany and the
descent of the Holy Spirit as the outbreak of any kind of
enthusiasm, then God could place other revelations alongside of this revelation.   If Jesus Christ and if the Holy
Ghost is no less God, no less the divine Subject Himself
than the God from Whom they come and to Whom they
witness, then the conception of a " second " revelation
is in itself impossible.   But indeed what this one unique
revelation in Christ through the Spirit reveals to us is
actually " that the *eternal* Father of our Lord *Jesus
Christ* . . . is, for the sake of Jesus Christ His Son,
my God and *my* Father " (Heidelberg Cat. Q. 26).

God is therefore in truth Father because and in so far
as He is in truth the Father of Jesus Christ and with Him
the source of the Holy Spirit.   Therefore and in so far
can He be and is He our Father.   It is *grace* and not
nature (the nature of the relationship of God and man,
already known to us) that we may call God " Father "
in virtue of the knowledge of His omnipotence.   As indeed this knowledge also itself rests on God's *revelation* of
His omnipotence.   But the grace that, in virtue of His
revelation of omnipotence, we dare know Him as Father
and call Him Father, itself again rests on the *truth* that
He in Himself from eternity to eternity is Father of the
Son and with Him source of the Holy Spirit, *fons et
origo totius divinitatis.*   God's Fatherhood is an eternal
" person," i.e. a peculiar eternal possibility and mode of
being ($\tau\rho\acute{o}\pi os$ $\acute{v}\pi\acute{a}\rho\xi\epsilon\omega s$) in God.   That this is so is a fact
that comes to us in the power of the act of omnipotence
by which we are taught to call Him our Father.   This
act has the full irresistible power of divine truth.   We say

the same thing when we say : it has the power of the eternal Word and of the eternal Spirit in relation to Whom God is the eternal Father. The revelation that God is our Father comes to us—if it does come to us—with the complete and incomparable downpouring of the inner, the trinitarian reality of God. Since God is the *eternal* Father, His power is *real* omnipotence, is that " Whence " of our existence and of our world that is absolutely commanding and compelling, and, just on that account, so consoling. He can be, as we shall hear later, the *Creator* of heaven and earth, and He is that because He is the *eternal* Father.

We conclude with some explanatory observations.

1. God's Fatherhood does not mean that there is in God's being a super- and sub-ordination, that the Father is God more and otherwise than the Son and the Holy Spirit. God, as the eternally Begotten of the Father, and God, as He Who proceeds eternally from the Father and from the Son are in the same way God as God the Father Himself. His being the Father does not indicate a superordination, but an order in God. So also God's revelation of the omnipotence is not something higher compared with God's revelation of grace ; God's revelation of grace in Jesus Christ is not merely to be understood as a form and manifestation of the paternal revelation of omnipotence. That could only be if, in contradiction to the testimony of Scripture, the eternal Godhead of the Son and of the Spirit and along with that God's eternal Fatherhood also were to be misunderstood.

2. God's Fatherhood does not signify a special separate part in the being of God, but a " person " or mode of being of the one simple divine being, of one substance with the Son and with the Spirit, and in His peculiarity

inseparably bound with them. Therefore the meaning cannot be that only the Father is Almighty and not also the Son and the Spirit—and that the Father is only Almighty and did not also share in all those attributes of God, of which the Second and the Third Articles of the symbol speak. *Opera trinitatis ad extra sunt indivisa.* It is impossible to prefer with the Enlightenment faith in the Father-God, or with Pietism to seek to practise Christocentric theology or even a special Spirit-theology without imperilling the sure path of truth and finally losing it.

3. Yet the knowledge of God the *Father* gained from the act of His revelation of *omnipotence* is not to be taken as a misunderstanding to be corrected in a higher knowledge, in order then to disappear. For the Father is not the Son and not the Holy Spirit, although the Son and the Holy Spirit are not without the Father. So He also in His revelation is, it is true, not without them, as they are not without Him, but in the unity and simplicity of the divine being He is yet precisely in His *omnipotence* precisely the *Father*. If the *activity* of God like His Being is a unity, it is nevertheless an ordered unity and in this order the reflection and repetition of the order of His *being*. The fact that we lay stress upon the knowledge of the " Father Almighty " as a special first knowledge of God, and that there is a special first Article of the Creed, is as much justified, indeed demanded by the knowledge of the eternity of the divine Fatherhood as that same knowledge must summon us to see the Almighty Father in His unity with the Son and the Spirit, and therefore also to understand the three Articles of the Creed as a unity.

IV

CREATOREM COELI ET TERRAE

THE doctrine of Creation turns our attention for the first time directly to a reality different from the reality of God, the reality of the *world*. This doctrine has, for all that, absolutely nothing to do with a " world view," even with a Christian world view. Nor is it any part of a *general science* that has got perhaps to be crowned and completed by Christian knowledge. If man looks at the world generally and from out of himself, and thinks he knows something of its origin, and if he perhaps decides to name this origin " God," he must yet turn round again and become as a child in order to hear and comprehend what the symbol in common with Holy Scripture says : Creator of heaven and earth. But again, it is *not* by any means a specifically " Christian " world view that the Creed offers us. The wording itself should warn us off this idea, for it does *not* speak (in analogy with the expressions of the second and third Articles) of a *creatio coeli et terrae*, and therefore of a *mundus a Deo creatus*, but—and that is something different—of the *creator coeli et terrae*. A statement is here made about *God*. Let it be carefully noted : about the same God of Whom we have just heard that He is, and in what sense He is, the " Almighty Father ". And *Creator* is the name here applied to God. Let it be carefully considered whether what people think they know generally and of themselves about an origin of the

28

world is not something quite different from what the word " Creation " implies. And it is " Creator of *heaven* and earth " that He is called. It must once more be carefully considered whether that which people think they are able generally and of themselves to say about Creator and creation does not perhaps merely amount to a description of the relationship in which heaven is superior to earth and that it has absolutely nothing to do with the creation of the world which comprehends heaven and earth (of all things visible *and* invisible, as the Nicene symbol supplements the statement). It has to be borne in mind that the word *credo* stands before the words *creatorem coeli et terrae.* " By *faith* we understand that the worlds were fashioned by the word of God " (Heb. xi. 3). By the very same word that has also got to be *said* to us in order that we may be able to know it.

The doctrine of creation, or more accurately, of the Creator, speaks of God in His relation to our existence as such and to our world. To that extent it could be said : it brings to its sharpest, most fundamental expression what the words " Father Almighty " already declared. The doctrine says not only that we are completely and absolutely bound, and that we completely and absolutely belong to God, the Almighty, the Lord over life and death, the Father of Jesus Christ, but it says that without Him we should not be, and that we exist only through Him. It says that our real existence stands or falls with God's giving it to us and maintaining it. There is much to be said for Luther's placing *man* at the centre of the created world, in his explanation of the first Article : " I believe that God has made *me* together with all creatures ". The fact that God made heaven and earth does indeed concern man, man who lives under heaven upon earth, himself at once a visible and an invisible being. But there is also much and perhaps more to be said for doing what the symbol itself does—for *not* expressly emphasising man as creation of God or bringing him right into the centre. Most decidedly the knowledge of God as the Creator and of man as His creature and therefore the knowledge of the difference between God and man and of their true relationship would not be subserved if man was going with excessive forwardness to look upon himself as, and to enjoy the experience of being, *the* creature and *the* partner of God. Will he recognise, fear and love God as God the Creator, without at the same time recognising, as he looks down to earth and up to heaven, his own littleness and insignificance, both in body and soul, even within the creaturely sphere ? Without indeed mentioning man, and significant in its failure to mention man, the statement that God created heaven and earth says the decisive thing even about him, and precisely about him. Of these *two* worlds he is the citizen, encompassed in truth with a special mystery, or the wanderer between these two worlds which indeed in God's sight are only *one* world, the created world.

The statement : " God is the Creator of the World " has in the main a double content : it speaks of the *freedom* of God (one could also say : of His *holiness*) over against the world, and of His *relationship* (one could also say : of His love) to the world.

1. With the proposition : God is the Creator ! we acknowledge that the relationship of God and world is fundamentally and in all its implications not one of equilibrium or of parity, but that in this relationship

30

God has the absolute *primacy*. This is no mere matter of course, but rather a mystery, which all along the line determines the meaning and the form of this relationship : that there is a reality at all differentiated from the reality of God, a being beside the divine Being. There is that. There are heaven and earth, and between the two, between angel and animal, man. But quite apart from the explicit proposition about Creation, for Scripturally based thinking there follows from the fact that their being is so closely related to the Being of God, this : that their being can only be one that is radically dependent on the Being of God, therefore one that is radically relative and without independence, dust, a drop in the bucket, clay in the hand of the potter—mere figures of speech which far from saying too much, say decidedly much too little. Heaven and earth are what they are *through* God and *only* through God. This brings us to the true thought of creation.

Heaven and earth are *not themselves God*, are not anything in the nature of a divine generation or emanation, are not, as the Gnostics or mystics would again and again have it, in some direct or indirect way, identical with the Son or Word of God. In opposition to what even Christian theologians have on occasion taught, the world must not be understood as eternal. It has, and with it time and space have, a *beginning*. Their infinity is not only limited by the finite as such. Rather, their infinity is, *along with* everything finite, limited and encompassed by God's eternity and omnipotence, i.e. by God's lordship over time and space, in which it itself does not share. Therefore the creation of the world is not a movement of God in Himself, but a free **opus ad extra**, finding its necessity only in His love, but again not casting any doubt on His self-sufficiency : the world cannot exist without God, but if God were not love (as such inconceivable !), He could exist very well without the world. " And all this out of pure paternal, divine goodness and mercy, without any merit or worthiness of mine," as again Luther says, speaking not yet of our salvation, but of our creation.

Again heaven and earth are not God's work in the sense that God created them according to some *ideas* in themselves given and true, or out of some *material* already existing, or by means of some *instrument* apt in itself for that purpose. Creation in the Bible sense means : Creation solely on the basis of God's own wisdom. It means, *creatio ex nihilo* (Rom. iv. 17). It means, creation by the word, which is indeed the eternal Son and therefore God Himself. If that is so, if there is no question of an identity of the created world with God, no question of its existing under any circumstances as a legitimate possibility (i.e. apart from sin) in formal or material independence over against God, then it necessarily follows that the *meaning* and the *end* of the world of His creation is not to be sought in itself, that the purpose and the destiny of this world could only be to serve God as the world's Creator and indeed to serve as " theatre of His glory " (Calvin). From God's creating the world it follows that He created it for *this* purpose and with this destiny and therefore created it in accordance with this purpose and this destiny and therefore *good*. Here we must of course acknowledge anew the primacy of God and must therefore in *our* estimate of the " goodness " of this world hold to the judgment of *God*. He knows what serves His glory. We must believe that the world as He created it is appointed to serve His glory, and we must not allow ourselves to be misled here by our feelings and reflections over good and evil, however justified. No doubt it is scriptural to say that the world was created for man's sake. But yet only because man was in a pre-eminent sense created for the service of God, created to be the " image of God," not only as theatre, but as active and passive bearer of that glory. It is the concrete content of faith in God the Creator that the world is " good " for man in and for this service of God. How should man have to decide and decree what is " good " ? He has just got to *believe* that God has created the world and him himself really *good*.

2. With the proposition : God is the Creator ! we now recognise also that just in that so utterly unequal relationship in which it stands to God, the world has *reality* and indeed a reality *of its own*, that is willed and appointed by God, upheld, accompanied and guided by God. The world having once been created by God (apart from sin !) cannot obviously cease to be determined by this decisive fact. It can no doubt cease to exist, should God will that it no longer exist. But as long as it exists, it cannot cease to be the God-created world. It cannot be a world forsaken by God, left to itself or to chance or to fate or to its own laws. Not as if it could not do that of itself ! In the world itself there are no eternal necessities, no eternal impossibilities. But it cannot do it because it is and remains true that God is its Creator. A sovereignty of chance, of fate, or of the world's own system of laws would be at variance with this truth. That is impossible. Because God is the Creator of the world, therefore it stands under His sovereignty, therefore there is a co-existence of Him and

33

it. It is the totally unequal co-existence of Creator and creature, a co-existence in strictest supremacy and subordination, but yet a co-existence, and therefore an existence of God not only in Himself, but also with and within the world, because it is, and in so far as it is, His creature. Therefore in the proposition, " God is the Creator," we recognise not only God's transcendence, but also the immanence of that God so completely transcendent to the world. Remembering the Creator's transcendence, we shall be safeguarded against ascribing to the world as such any divinity whether imparted to it by God or belonging to itself independently. This very same recollection of the Creator's transcendence will, however, also warn us against denying God's co-existence with the world and therefore His immanence, i.e. His free omnipotent presence and lordship in the world that He created. God never and nowhere becomes world. The world never and nowhere becomes God. God and world remain over against each other. The limit of this statement must not be forgotten : the Word of God in the flesh. Within that limit this statement certainly holds. But in standing over against the World that He has made, God is *present* to it—not only far, but also *near*, not only free in relation to it, but *bound* to it, not only transcendent, but also *immanent*. Here there can be no question of any conception of transcendence to be defined by logic. We are concerned with the transcendence of God the Creator. The knowledge of that compels the recognition of His immanence also.—The old Dogmatics handled this side of the doctrine of Creation under the title *De providentia,* of divine Providence. I can reproduce its content here only very briefly. To the world (also to man !) as His creature

34

God the Creator is present in this way, that He maintains it in its relative independence and peculiar character, in its reality which differs from His reality ; but at the same time also, as the absolutely supreme Lord, He accompanies and therefore rules the world in whole and in part, according to His divine will and pleasure, without totally or even partly abolishing the contingency of the creature, or the freedom of the human will. The Pelagian doctrine of freedom and the fatalistic doctrine of necessity, the indeterminism of the old Lutherans and Molinists and the determinism of Zwingli (which also, if I see aright, was still in 1525 that of Luther !) represent in what are fundamentally similar ways misreadings of that freedom in which providence recognises, encompasses and governs the contingency of the creature, the freedom of the human will as such. The school of Calvin has here shown the lines along which we can " understand," on the one hand, the reality that belongs to the created world, without exalting it to be a god alongside of God, and on the other hand, the sovereignty of God, without taking from the created world its reality.

But the doctrine of Creation has its definite *limits* which have got to be known if that doctrine is to be rightly understood. God is no doubt even as Creator the one God in His totality, Father, Son and Holy Spirit, but in knowing God, Who is Father, Son and Holy Spirit, as *Creator*, we can only partly know Him. The first Article of the Creed must necessarily be followed by the second and the third. I conclude with pointing to these limits. There are again two things to which we have to pay attention :—

1. There are definite and necessary *questions* of faith which are not to be answered from the doctrine of

creation, or at least not unequivocally and completely. Such is the question about the possibility of *sin* as the act in which, in defiance of the sovereignty of God, the creature arrogates to himself not only his own reality but independent reality, an absolute independence, and therefore makes himself God. Further, the question about the possibility of *evil*, i.e. of such experiences as notoriously are not to man's highest advantage in spite of the goodness of the world made by God, as do not conduce to God's being glorified by man, but rather the reverse. Finally, the question about the possibility of *death* as such an end of creaturely existence as, despite the sustaining grace of divine forbearance, means its precipitation into the void. These three questions, known by the name of the Problem of Theodicy, could be concentrated into the question about the possibility which the *Devil* had, and has, to be the Devil. From the viewpoint of the dogma of creation it is no doubt possible to answer with the assertion that God as the Creator of the world in its true reality which is determined by Him, is the supreme Lord and Victor also over these absurd, these impossible possibilities. But it cannot be said that God willed and created these possibilities also as such. The seriousness of the questions which are raised in view of these possibilities, the whole reality and the whole character of sin, evil, death and the devil would, with Schleiermacher and many others be misapprehended, or God would, with Zwingli, be turned into an incomprehensible tyrant, if these possibilities were to be included in the work of divine creation, and consequently justified as appointed and willed by God. In order to keep true to the facts, Dogmatics has here, as in other places, to be logically inconsequent.

Therefore in spite of the *omnipotence* of God—or rather on the score of the rightly understood omnipotence of *God*, Dogmatics must not at this place carry the Creation-thought right to the end of the line. It must rather explain those possibilities as being such that we have indeed to reckon most definitely with their reality, but are unable better to describe their real nature and character than by forbearing to ask for their *raison d'être* either in the will of God the Creator or even with Marcion and the Manicheans in the will of a wicked Anti-God. These possibilities are to be taken seriously as the *mysterium iniquitatis.* The existence of such a thing, however, is not to be perceived from creation, but only from the grace of God in Jesus Christ.

2. But there are also definite and equally necessary *answers* of faith, which also admit of being ranged, though likewise not satisfactorily, within the framework of the knowledge of God the Creator. There is *miracle* as the event in which in an extraordinary manner the order of the world, destroyed by sin, evil, death and devil, is temporarily restored by God Himself, as an accompanying sign of His revelation. *Prayer*, in which man not only speaks with God, but in spite of sin, evil, death and devil is heard and answered by God, and, incomprehensibly, with and in spite of all difference between Creator and creature, with the will of God has part in determining the will of God. Finally, the *Church* as the place where, in the midst of the dominion of sin, evil, death and devil, there is proclaimed and accepted a special presence of God, the presence of God in His revelation in contradistinction to the presence of God the Creator, which, in spite of everything, cannot and must not be denied to the rest of human history and

society. All these are in any case very special forms of divine immanence in the world. In view of these things our forefathers were in the habit of speaking of *providentia speciallissima.* And these things pass beyond our range of vision because they are all bound up with the central mystery of the Incarnation, which is most assuredly misunderstood if with Schleiermacher it is understood as the completion and crown of creation. It is not that in Christ creation has reached its goal, but that in Christ the Creator has become—and this is something different—Himself creature ; the creature has been assumed into unity with the Creator as first-fruits of a *new* creation. Projecting our thought " consequently " along the line of the creation dogma, we should have in one way or another to deny the Incarnation, Miracle, prayer, the Church. That has often enough been done. But the facts demand that we give it up, though consistency seems to demand it. In truth it is just in the knowledge of Jesus Christ that we stand at the *source* of the creation, faith and dogma. If we did not know about the immanence, once and for all and in an altogether special sense, of the Word of God in the flesh, how would and could we dare, in despite of sin, evil, death and devil, to believe in a general immanence of God in the world, and to live ? Therefore far from our having to, or being able to, deny the former for the sake of the latter, we have to acknowledge the former in order rightly to believe and teach the latter.

V

ET IN JESUM CHRISTUM, FILIUM EIUS UNICUM

WITH these words we step into the great centre of the Christian Creed. And here decisions are made. For instance, our understanding of the second Article decides whether we rightly understand the first and the third, and therefore whether we understand the whole as *Christian* creed in its true nature and distinct from all other actual and possible creeds. Whether a sermon and proclamation in word or writing have rightly or wrongly a place in the Christian *Church* is decided by their relationship to the second article. At this point Dogmatics, as watchman, cannot be too wide-awake. Besides, even its own fate is here decided, namely, in the question whether it is genuinely Church *Theology*, because bound to the exegesis of the Holy Scriptures as witness to revelation, or on the other hand a Philosophy, working with Biblical and Church materials under another sovereignty altogether. The decision that is here made is of course not a human, but a divine and therefore ultimately hidden, decision. That is the proviso under which human, even Christian judgment will here also have to bow. Even by the decisive clauses to which we shall now turn, we are called neither to be judges over ourselves nor to be judges over others, but we *are* called to watch. That proviso does not one whit alter the fact that here in a special way decisions are made. Just on that account we shall here also have to be in a very special sense awake.

The arrangement of the three Articles is not to be understood genetically, i.e. it does not represent the way in which faith gets its knowledge. If that had been intended, then undoubtedly the second Article would have had to be the first. Perhaps there were very old forms of the symbol which actually had this structure. In 2 Cor. xiii. 13, we hear the sequence : " the grace of the Lord Jesus Christ, the love of God, the communion of the Holy Spirit ". If the symbol in its later form, according to Matt. xxviii. 19 ; Rom. i. 1-4 ; xi. 33 ; 2 Thess. ii. 13, puts it differently, it is clearly intended to set forth the *essential* order, the way of God's condescension, which is the content of revelation : in the first Article God who, as Father, is over man, in the second, God Who, as Son, Himself becomes man, in the third, God Who, as Holy Spirit, is with man. But even if this that the symbol sets before us is the essential order, the second Article belongs to the *beginning* of the order of our *knowing*. The " Father Almighty, Creator of heaven and earth " Who, according to the first Article, is over man, is none other than the Father of Jesus Christ ; and likewise God the Holy Spirit Who, according to the third Article, is with man, is the Spirit of this Father and of this Son. If God had not become man, as is recognised and confessed in the second Article, then everything we could conceive and say to ourselves about God *over* man and about God *with* man, would hang in the air as arbitrarily, as mistakenly and as misleadingly, as the corresponding ideas which, in the long run, have been fashioned about God and man in all religions and cosmic speculations. And therefore the fact to which the second Article bears witness, namely that

God became man, must be absolutely determinative for us for the interpretation of the first and third. As there is no special and direct revelation of the Father and Creator as such, so also there is no special and direct revelation of the Spirit. But the revelation of the Son is as such at once the revelation of the Father and of the Spirit.

The second Article begins by naming as object of the *credo* a man, " *Jesus,*" and at once goes on to identify this man, by means of the designation, " *Christ,*" with the prophet, priest and king of the last days, expected by the people of Israel, in order then, by means of the expression " God's only Son," to place Him in the closest relationship, indeed, in unity, with God Himself. Here above all we shall have to marvel if we are to understand. What does Jesus here signify ? What does he signify here as Messiah of Israel ? What does he signify, this Jesus, the Christ, in proximity to God and as apparently second object of the *credo ?* Here it is justifiable, here we are bound to wonder. In the first Article we heard of the concealment of God : here we are told that He has form and indeed a quite definite form. We heard there of His omnipotence ; here we are told about a special act of God on the narrow strip of human history upon which a prophecy given to the people of Israel is to reach fulfilment. We heard there that God is the Creator ; here we are told, if we only rightly understand, that He Himself is creature too, that He is not only Lord of our existence, but that He is here with us and like us. We heard there of His unity ; here we are told of a difference within this unity, namely, of a unique Son of God, unique in the sense that He clearly exists as such uniquely, and that He only is so to be named. One surprise and difficulty here follows on the heels of another. And again, anyone who perhaps understood the doctrines of divine omnipotence and creation as abstract truths—that is, abstracted from the fact that the Almighty Father and Creator is the Father of Jesus Christ—would no doubt be brought to a halt here, and, either, in face of what is here said, refuse to go on, or, on the other hand, would have to reinterpret what is here said with the utmost violence, in order to make it acceptable to himself. But even if we go on together, and indeed go on together without reinterpretation, we shall at all events have to say : Here actually begins a second, another, an amazing new Article of the Christian knowledge of God.

In order to answer the question here put to us, reference can, and indeed must, be made to the abyss of that enigma which we briefly touched on at the end of the last Lecture with the words sin, evil, death and devil. The second Article—it would then be said—is the testimony of revelation and Christian faith in face of this enigma. It speaks of the reconciliation accomplished in Jesus Christ as the incarnate Word of God ; accomplished in His passion, death and resurrection, in execution of His Messianic office as prophet, priest and king, the reconciliation of sinful man, i.e. man who has fallen from unity of will with his Creator and who has thereby fallen under the sway of evil and death and finally under that impossibility in person, the devil. That is actually the case ; the second Article does speak of this reconciliation ; and therefore the attempt has again and again been made of old and in recent times to establish and explain the doctrine of Jesus Christ and thereby the decisive centre of the Christian creed on this basis, namely, by reference to the negative precondition of this reconciliation, by opening up as sharply, emphatically, seriously as possible the gulf between God and man which has been bridged by Jesus Christ as reconciler. The misery and despair of man, who has become guilty before God and who therefore stands under God's judgment, give the light by which are to be recognised what grace is and Who Jesus Christ is, namely, God's only Son. But it will be necessary to have at least a very good idea of what one is about, in saying that, and so in seeking to establish and explain the revelation of Christ on that basis. The first thing that must strike us as remarkable is that the Creed itself has *not* considered it necessary to prefix to the doctrine of Christ, by way of basis and explanation, a special doctrine of sin and death. In that it follows Holy Scripture, which likewise neither in the Old Testament nor in the New speaks at the outset abstractly of the misery and the despair of man, in order then to show against this background that God is gracious to man and how gracious He is. Although undoubtedly Creed and Scriptures alike are of the opinion that God's grace in Jesus Christ is the answer to this misery and this despair! Yet they speak really and properly solely of that answer, and only incidentally of the question—only incidentally of man's sin and punishment, strictly speaking, however seriously they regard them. Jesus Christ is the background from which man's misery and despair receive their light and not vice versa. What is the significance of that? Clearly this : there is, so to speak, an unfruitful knowledge of sin, of evil, of death and the devil, that succeeds in making it hard for a man to have happy and confident faith in the Almighty Father and Creator, but without making possible for him, or even bringing nearer, faith in Jesus Christ as reconciler. To gaze down into that abyss, as far as it is possible for us to do that of ourselves, does not in itself help us in the least, so frightful is the abyss! *How* frightful it is no man has ever yet fathomed of himself. What man has in this respect fathomed of himself has been nothing but puppet sins and puppet distresses, that are far removed from being the actual problem of Theodicy in all its awfulness. Grace must come first, in order that sin may be manifest to us as sin, and death as death; in order that, with the Heidelberg Catechism (Q. 5), we may confess that we are by nature prone to hate God and our neighbour, and therefore, with Luther, that we are lost and damned men. We cannot of ourselves know what our misery and our despair, our guilt and punishment really are; that becomes manifest to us in the fact that Christ has taken them upon Himself and borne them. But if that does become manifest to us—namely, in the answer which *God* has already given to our state, before *we* ourselves knew of it, in the Cross of Jesus Christ, in the depth of the mercy that is shown to us in Him—if we come into the judgment of *grace*, which alone has the power to install the law (as Gal. iii. 24 puts it) as our pedagogue, then we will recognise and praise this pedagogy of the law, given and revealed to us by grace—this pedagogy that is the way into despair and out of despair into consolation, the way to the knowledge of our guilt and punishment, and, with this knowledge, into the place of God, out of the power of the devil into the power of God— we shall recognise and praise this pedagogy, not at all as our self-pedagogy, not as our way but as God's way. And therefore it is not from any arbitrary absorption in our own wickedness and distress that we expect knowledge of Jesus Christ, but on the contrary it is only from knowledge of Jesus Christ as the " author and perfecter of our faith " (Heb. xii. 2) that we look for knowledge of the law

44

and with it wholesome knowledge of our sin, guilt and punishment. Sin scorches us when it comes under the light of forgiveness, not before. Sin scorches us then by becoming visible as our enmity against God, and therefore by compelling us, as our thoughts start out from that, at last to put the question properly : How is that possible which the second Article states ? If it can appear to us almost impossible that the *Creator* became *creature*, it must appear to us *absolutely* impossible that the Holy One, Whose burning wrath we have evoked, became *man* in order, in spite of everything, to befriend us. If He has really done that, and if this is the central content of Christian faith, then we cannot explain and establish it from elsewhere and least of all by an analysis of our distress and despair ; then we can understand it (and consequently the central content of the Christian faith) only as the occurrence of a revelation of *grace*, which is beyond all our understanding because it makes possible what is absolutely impossible, *to* which our knowledge cannot attain, and *from* which it can always only derive.

It is in this way and in this sense—that is, deriving from an occurrence that cannot be understood from elsewhere but only out of itself—that the Creed begins the second Article. It is in this way and in the same sense that prophecy in the Old Testament, and its fulfilment in Jesus Christ in the New Testament, are attested. If the attempt is made to understand and interpret the witness of apostles and prophets in the light of human ideas as human explanation of human action, then even in a purely historical-exegetical treatment one self-deception and *aporia* follows another. They themselves at any rate did not so understand it. Even when they used the language of human ideas and were looking at a human action, their intention was to speak of a divine initiative among men, something that was to be understood as such and not as human action and human idea. The Old Testament calls this divine initiative the making known of the name of the Lord. The New Testament names it Jesus Christ. Yes, indeed, here is cause to marvel. Here the hidden, the eternal and incomprehensible God has taken visible form. Here the Almighty is mighty in a quite definite, particular, earthly happening. Here the Creator Himself has become creature and therefore objective reality. Here in His Son, in the revelation of His Name and Word, the one God has shown Himself as differentiated in Himself, so that we can hear Him, so that we can say " Thou " to Him as to one of ourselves. It is revelation in this strict, firm, literal sense that Scripture and the Confession mean when they bear witness to Jesus Christ. And the sense of this revelation becomes even stricter and firmer when this too is added—that here the abyss is bridged, that here, in and with this revelation, our reconciliation is accomplished, that this Jesus Christ is *God for us*, for us His incarnation, for us His existence as true God and true man, for us everything that later is said of Him from His birth of the Virgin Mary up to His return in judgment. In fact, what we are concerned with is that absolute impossibility, that the Holy One, Whose wrath we have provoked, became man, in order, in spite of everything, to befriend us, to bear this wrath Himself and in our place, accordingly to suffer in our place His own burning wrath, to give satisfaction Himself in our place, in order in that way to be *our* God (and that means, to be *good* for us in a way that we have not deserved and cannot comprehend), He Himself, directly and personally our Prophet, Priest and King. Again, neither historical facts nor ideas nor even their insight into the depth of human wickedness and distress, made the prophets and apostles, if we are to trust themselves, witnesses to Jesus Christ, but simply and solely this concentrated event of revelation and reconciliation that could not be prognosticated from anywhere because it was unexpected and in its divinity only to be acknowledged. Even the knowledge of the abyss between God's good creation and our actual state was for them included as a *supplementary* cognition in and only in that event. In the mind of the prophets and apostles, then, the question of faith in Jesus Christ cannot be the question of the Why ? of this event, but only the question of our decision as its actuality confronts us.

The decision of faith, however, in face of this event, as *faith's* decision gets its character through what the symbol expresses in the further words : " God's only Son ". Faith in the sense of the symbol and of the Holy Scriptures can only be faith in God. The designation of Jesus Christ as " the only Son of God " says that He Himself is *God*, God's *Son*, but as only Son of God no other than the one and only God *Himself*. It is notorious that this knowledge, so far as its accurate definition is concerned, is the result of the work which the Church of the first centuries had to perform in conflict with the heathen interpretations of the Christian creed. Only from the fourth century onwards were those formulæ established which were to secure this knowledge against diverse views that sound similar but that point in a completely different direction. Even the Biblical expression " God's only Son " could be understood and has been understood in the sense of a heathen religious view—as if faith in Jesus Christ referred to a divine intermediate being subordinate

47

to God. According to the so-called Nicæno-Constantino-politan symbol these safeguarding formulæ run : that the Son was begotten of the Father before all time, begotten not made, that He therefore is of one substance with the Father ("God of God, Light of Light, very God of very God "), that by Him all things were made. Thereby dogma was only confirming the self-evident presupposition of the Biblical testimony, namely, that that event, to which it bears testimony, is an initiative which takes place neither in human history nor in human thought— to speak with the first article : neither in earth nor in heaven, but in God Himself. He does not reveal Himself through another. He reveals Himself through Himself. And He Who reconciles us with Himself in this revelation, the Holy One Who makes His dwelling here among sinners to be the sinners' Saviour is again no lesser, no other than the eternal God Himself. So deep is the abyss—now it becomes clear how deep it is—which separates us from Him, that to bridge it nothing less than God Himself will suffice. But God Himself does it, and in doing it shows that He *can* do it, because He *is* the triune God, the Father of the *Son*, the Son of the *Father*, both of these not only in His revelation, not only in His reconciling us with Himself, but both of these in truth and power in His revelation and reconciliation, because from eternity to eternity He is none other than just this God.

Care should be taken to avoid regarding this pre-supposition of the Biblical witness (which after all Dogma does no more than make explicit), as a metaphysic super-fluous and alien to Christian faith, and therefore getting rid of or emasculating it. The Theology of modern Protestantism has done that again and again. This modern Protestantism has punished itself with the most varied and disastrous relapses into just those heathen religious views which the Church fathers of the first centuries rightly and successfully resisted. It can be asserted and proved with the utmost definiteness and accuracy that the great theological-ecclesiastical catastrophe of which the German Protestantism of the moment is the arena, would have been impossible if the three words *Filium eius unicum* in the properly understood sense of the Nicene trinitarian doctrine had not for more than two hundred years been really lost to the German Church amongst a chaos of reinterpretations designed to make them innocuous. This catastrophe should be a real, final warning to the evangelical Churches, and, especially to the theological faculties of other lands, where, so far as trinitarian dogma is concerned, no better ways are being trodden. Christian faith stands or falls once and for all with the fact that God and God alone is its object. If one rejects the Biblical doctrine that Jesus Christ is God's Son, and indeed God's only Son, and that therefore the whole revelation of God and all reconciliation between God and man is contained in Him—and if one then, in spite of that, speaks of " faith " in Jesus Christ, then one believes in an intermediate being, and *then* consequently one is really pursuing metaphysics and has already secretly lapsed from the Christian faith into a polytheism which will forthwith mature into further fruits in the setting up of a special God-Father faith and a special Creator faith, and in the assertion of special spiritual revelations. The proclamation of this polytheism can most certainly be a brilliant and a pleasant affair, and can win continuous and widespread approbation. But real consolation and real instruction, the Gospel of God and the Law of God, will find a small and ever-diminishing place in this proclamation. The Church of Jesus Christ as the assembly of lost and rescued sinners will come less and less to be built by this proclamation. How could it be otherwise than that error at a crucial point makes it utterly impotent ? It is just here that a circumspect Dogmatics will give warning. It will have to ask the whole Church to consider that the ground out of which it has sprung and out of which alone it is able to live, is the admittedly rigid and uncompromising recognition that no one knows the Son, but the Father, and no one knows the Father, save the Son, and he to whom the Son will reveal Him (Matt. xi. 27).

VI

DOMINUM NOSTRUM

WITH these words we can at once prove the correctness of what was last said. The designation of Jesus Christ as the Lord has no doubt never yet been seriously questioned in the Christian Church. Anyone who wanted to do that would have to set himself in downright opposition to many hundreds of New Testament passages. But what is the meaning of " Lord " ? There are many lords in the world. If Jesus is one of the many lords in the world, if fundamentally He is lord only in the same way as other lords can be, then it is not possible to see by what decisive necessity just He and He alone should be " our Lord ". Then it is to be assumed that many another lord is only waiting to make known and to enter upon his lordship over us. Then it is probably to be assumed that while we call Jesus Christ our Lord, we have, whether consciously or unconsciously, had in addition, for long and in the most varied spheres, quite different lords. The confession " Jesus Christ our Lord " is then a perhaps quite sincere and piously meant confession, but it is fundamentally polytheistic. Our belief in this Lord is accordingly no more than any of those good, sincere, pious beliefs that are to be found in the world. And so also the proclamation of this Lord is no more than a solemn utterance such as can quite regularly be evoked in this world by solemn occasions.

But there can be no question that long before the Council of Nicæa the designation of Jesus Christ as the Lord, in the symbol and in those hundreds of New Testament passages, was differently and indeed fundamentally differently meant than in that way. The New Testament witnesses knew as well as anyone else, what indeed no one can deny : that there are many lords in the world, petty but also great, bad but also good. The Apostle Paul especially reckoned with that fact quite soberly and frankly. But when nevertheless he proceeds to call Jesus Christ the *one* Lord (1 Cor. viii. 6), he does not by that merely place Him at the top of the pyramid of these many lords, and therefore really at their side, but he expressly places Him at the side of the one *Father*. To be Lord in the sense in which Paul uses that term of Jesus Christ means, according to the same passage, to be that One by Whom all things were made. It means, to be Creator in the same way in which that is attributed to the Father. To the glory of God the Father, so we read in Phil. ii. 10 f., *every* knee should bow, of things in heaven, and things on earth, and things under the earth, and every tongue confess just this : that Jesus Christ is Lord. That reaches out clearly and consciously beyond the sense in which in the contemporary Hellenistic religions a cult-god, for example, could be called " lord " of the members of the cult in question, or the Roman Emperor " lord " of the Empire conceived as comprehensive cult-association. *Every* knee, *every* tongue, and these words are meant to include expressly all creation in its heights and in its depths. Only *one* parallel from the history of religion can in this connection be seriously considered, the usual Greek translation of the Old Testament name of God. Kurios means Jahweh. But just this parallel absolutely forbids us to understand the designation "Lord" other than strictly monotheistically. The New Testament furnished outwardly and inwardly the basis for the addition in the Nicænum of the word *unum* to the word *Dominum* whereby the whole designation was brought into line with those formulæ designed to safeguard the knowledge of the Godhead of Christ. *Lord*ship of Christ means *God*head of Christ.

But the reverse also may and indeed must interest us : *God*head of Christ means *Lord*ship of Christ.

The reproach has been levelled at the Apostolicum that it was kept so strangely objective and historical that actually in the second Article it says scarcely anything about a subject so very decisive for evangelical faith as the practical significance that the Person and the Work of Jesus Christ have for the life of His people. If that observation were correct, then Luther would have been guilty of a forced reinterpretation of the Apostolicum when he made the words " our Lord " the clue for his exposition of the second Article and understood these words in this way : " I believe that Jesus Christ . . . is my Lord, Who has redeemed me . . . in order that I might be His own, live under Him in His kingdom and serve Him. . . ." But just in view of the fact that the formula " Jesus Christ our Lord " was perhaps the original form of the whole Creed, at any rate one of its oldest parts, we dare not say that Luther made a mistake, even from the historical point of view, in bringing into the forefront this formula which, without doubt, is practically of the very highest value. If its contents only are considered— naturally on the just-mentioned assumption that the word " Lord " has here the full weight of the word " God " —then it shows itself in fact not only as the common denominator and key for all that is later said of Christ, but also at the same time as putting into the life (i.e. the ethical) relationship all that is said about Christ. With the words " *Dominum nostrum* " the content not only of the second Article but of the whole symbol is in fact set directly over against the word *credo*. With these words this *credo* is *filled out* as acknowledgment of a divine decision upon human existence, but it itself—being the actual acknowledgment of this decision—is also *formed* as a religious, as an ethical, yes, as a political decision of the man who says seriously, *credo*. How could it be otherwise, if it is true that we believe in Jesus Christ as our *Lord* ?

That Jesus Christ is our Lord means first of all that He has the authority and power over us that a Lord has over his servants. He taught them as one having ἐξουσία, authority, power, freedom over them (Matt. vii. 29). He has a claim on us, He commands, He rules and disposes of us. But " servants " in Scripture are always slaves : they belong to their lord ; they have no rights of their own, are not independent persons over against him ; they act not on their own responsibility, but strictly under his. He has paid for them to pass from the possession and service of another into his. So he is interested in them as his own property. Their preservation is his concern. And it is now that the assumption comes into force that the name " Lord," applied to Jesus, is identical with the name of God. This assumption extends the conception of lordship in a sense of which it is not humanly possible for us to form an idea. All human lordship has a human beginning ; it is a lordship that is derivative, that came into being at a point of time, and to that extent has no inevitable hold upon our existence. The Lordship of

54

Christ, however, is the Lordship of the Creator of our life, and, something far beyond that, of the Creator, yes the owner, of our new life as the life of those who in Him have been saved from sin and death. Therefore whether we recognise it as such or not, it is the Lordship that directly affects and embraces our very existence, a Lordship of such a nature that we cannot appeal against it to any higher court, because without it we should not exist, or if we did exist, should be lost. Further, all human lordship is limited inwardly by the servants' freedom of thought, of conscience, of heart. It is always a case of execrable tyranny when human lordship does not respect this limit, when it does not set up this limit for itself in order to be proper lordship. But the Lordship of Christ insists on being really and properly His Lordship—and up to this point there is no rest—in our free and most secret thoughts, His Lordship not only over our words and deeds, but over our hearts and consciences. Finally, all human lordship has a term and end—even if nothing else than the death of the ruled—beyond which it will assuredly not go with them. Praise and thanks be to God for that ! we shall say, since no human lordship has ever yet substantiated the claim to complete control of man, that is, as lordship over life and death. But of the Lordship of Christ the saying holds good, legitimately holds good : " He shall reign over the house of Jacob for ever, and of His kingdom there shall be no end " (Luke i. 33). For in contrast to all other lordships, it is the only true and the only effective Lordship. As βασιλεία τοῦ θεοῦ it is the kingdom of which all other kingdoms are only paltry and distorted adumbrations. It therefore abides, while all the mighty (rightly, all of them !) are being put down from their seats (Luke i. 52). Its subjects, if they really know the things which belong to their peace, will constantly require to pray and plead for its being established ever afresh : Thy Kingdom come !

From these remarks we see that over against this Lordship that we acknowledge with the word *credo* there remains for us no hiding-place, be it ever so worthy, ever so beautiful, yes, ever so pious.

We cannot, for example, separate our bodily existence from our psychical in order then to make the Lordship of Christ merely psychical and therefore internal, spiritual, invisible. As Creator of heaven and earth Christ is Lord of the whole man and is either recognised as such or not at all.

Again, we cannot, either in despair or in defiance, understand our natural existence as a whole, understand the field of human culture—and lack of culture—upon which we have our being, as a sphere in which prevail other laws and orders than in the sphere where we stand as sinners before the God of grace. The Lordship of Christ is not only a so-called religious Lordship ; as that, it is very much an ethical, yes, a political Lordship. " The field is the world " (Matt. xiii. 38). And just in our natural existence with all its real and alleged necessities we as sinners stand in a position of responsibility, whatever that may mean in detail, before the God of grace.

Further, we cannot expect to satisfy this Lordship with some extraordinary enthusiasm, be it ever so deep, sincere and vital. It demands obedience. No doubt it operates in the Spirit. But this Spirit is not any spirit, but the Spirit of Christ. " If any man have Him not, he is none of His " (Rom. viii. 9). And it does not rest with us to decide whether the spirit that drives us is the Spirit of Christ. That He Himself decides in person. We shall have to keep questioning Him as to how matters stand with the spirit by which *we* are bring driven. We shall have to keep seeking after *His* Spirit in His *Word*. We shall have to keep *asking* Him for *His* Spirit.

Further, we are not recognising His Lordship if we arbitrarily let one of its elements function in order openly or secretly to withdraw ourselves from another.—We cannot, for example, confine ourselves to merely accepting consolation from Christ from His promise that in Him our sins are forgiven and therefore eternal life is assured. That would certainly be a " filled-out " but not a " formed " *credo*, and as such not the *credo* that is determined by this Lordship. Such a limitation would mean an arbitrary treatment of this Lordship involving us not merely in partial but complete withdrawal from it. We cannot blind ourselves to the truth that Christ's Lordship signifies that we are in fact set free, which, however, means, set free from a false service to the true service (Rom. vi. 19), and that we are justified in Christ in order as such to have ourselves sanctified, i.e. awakened, claimed, bound and led. We shall not be able to deny that with the Gospel we have also heard the Law. Unless it be that we have not heard the Gospel itself, that with God's wrath God's righteousness in Christ was also revealed for us in vain.—Again, we cannot limit ourselves to accept from Christ merely commands and instructions for the formation of our life. That, on the other hand, would be truly a formed, but not a filled-out *credo* and, as such, just as little the *credo* determined by the Lordship of Christ. In this restriction, too, there is an arbitrariness of attitude to this Lordship that is crucial and utterly destructive. We are certainly not those who are able to hear the commands of Christ before they have first, by acceptance of the forgiveness of sins, had their whole existence and all their past and future works placed under the judgment and the grace of God. If we have not died with Christ, we cannot possibly live with Him. If we have not heard the Gospel, we shall never hear the Law. The law that we think we hear without the Gospel is certainly not God's Law. We shall then certainly not be able to fulfil God's Law, not because it is too hard and grievous for us, but because we do not yet know it. If we knew it, we should cling to Christ in Whom it is fulfilled, and in dependence on grace and in utter self-renunciation, should take upon ourselves the " easy yoke," the " light burden " (Matt. xi. 30) of His commands and instructions, to hold which is not grievous ! (1 John v. 3).

The great comprehensive temptation, danger and distress with which faith is assailed in relation to the Lordship of Christ consists finally in this—that, while we have perhaps very rightly understood it in its totality claim, we so easily confound and interchange it with our own lordship. Christian faith is verily, as long as time lasts, faith in the midst of temptation. The temptation is just for the Christian with his *credo* to proceed suddenly or imperceptibly, to form and fill out this *credo* of his himself, instead of leaving it to form and fill out. This is faith's temptation : that suddenly it can become lost, i.e. can come to regard itself as a human undertaking, work, exploit and system, to which Christ merely supplies a signature passionately invoked, but by which He has for long been rejected and crucified afresh for the sake of an ideal, an ideal that certainly implies a control over the whole man,—yes, even over the whole world, an ideal, moreover, that makes complete provision for prayer, for a proper relationship of justification and sanctification, for

Law and Gospel, and which yet is no more than a caricature and travesty of the Lordship of Christ. For what has actually happened is that man has made himself master, would like under the signature " Jesus Christ " to become himself a complete whole, would like himself to speak the creative word and be the living Spirit, would like himself to forgive sins and sanctify himself. And what makes this temptation so grave is the fact that this from top to bottom arbitrary human faith looks as like the real Christian faith that originates and lives under the Lordship of Christ as one egg is like another. Only that sooner or later, suddenly or gradually, but quite surely it suffers shipwreck, loses itself in some piece of folly or, what is almost worse, in trivialities of various kinds like a shrinking stream in the sand, if it does not degenerate into despair and unbelief. In this way or in that it must unmask itself as deception. An event that is the more painful and disastrous that it is not certain whether the individual observes in good time that what has suffered shipwreck is by no means the Christian faith but just the arbitrary human faith that pretended to be Christian. That is the temptation which in the life of individuals as in the life of the Church has of old and in later times been the enigma of much noticeable or hidden Christian stagnation and failure. That has got to be known. The Lordship of Christ is really the Lordship of *Christ!* The man who seriously wants to be a Christian cannot be sufficiently alert, cannot take himself sufficiently to task, as to whether perhaps he has not already or again subjected Lordship of Christ to his own lordship. If that were so, then there would be no cause for wonder at the occurrence sooner or later of a catastrophe to his alleged faith. The only way to repel and overcome this temptation is, in opposition to everything, absolutely everything that one thinks one knows of Christ and has of Him, to let the alone genuine and healing ἐξουσία of Jesus Christ Himself come anew before the eye. And that is best done by returning as beginner and learner again and again to the testimonies of prophets and apostles as the documents of the Lordship that is really *His*, relinquishing all, absolutely all Christian convictions, opinions and mental ruts, no matter how familiar and dear. There in the school of prophets and apostles humiliation is certainly tc be found, and then, as certainly, new encouragement also. But if encouragement is to be found there and the lesson learned no more to exchange the Christian faith for its double and namesake (as miserable as it is dangerous), then the humiliation must at no price be evaded. The two, faith and its double, can be distinguished by the voice of the Lord Himself and by that voice alone. We must keep listening to the voice of the Lord Himself.

We conclude with a brief note on the expression : Jesus Christ *our* Lord. Luther does not give the full meaning when in his catechism he makes a " my " out of this " our ". The " our " tells us that the life (i.e. the ethical) relationship of the testimony to Christ in the symbol and in Holy Scripture, in effect this Lordship of Christ, is no private intercourse between Christ and individual believers, but the rule of Christ in His *Church*. In the *congregation* of those called to Christian faith Christ is acknowledged and honoured as the Lord. That is done in the congregation, and even by individual Christians fundamentally *only* there. The fact that Christ becomes the Lord of my whole life is not something that I can have alone. I can have neither the Gospel nor the Law by myself. I can neither be justified by myself nor sanctified by myself. Moreover, I cannot overcome faith's great temptation alone and by myself. Only in the " Body of Christ " can I have all that, only in the midst of those who are constituted my brothers and sisters by the fact that they have heard and hear God's word along with me, that they witness to God's word for me, and on their part want, and must have, my witness to God's word : in the Church. The Lordship of Christ is rule of our life in that it is the rule of the Church, in that in the Church there is proper teaching and Baptism and Holy Communion all rightly administered, in that in the Church one serves the other " according as God hath dealt to every man the measure of faith " (Rom. xii. 3), in that the Church is drawn ever anew to new confession of His Name. Jesus Christ is *our* Lord. We listen there to something which no alleged knowledge of God from nature and history, something which no spirit of our own could say impressively and compellingly as the sum of all ethics : that it is only along with, and in responsibility towards, my neighbour that I can really stand before God and vindicate myself in His sight.

VII

QUI CONCEPTUS EST DE SPIRITU SANCTO, NATUS EX MARIA VIRGINE

THE confession " Jesus Christ God's only Son, our Lord " becomes possible and necessary in view of the objective event spoken of by the passage of the symbol that engages our attention to-day. On that account we have already had to refer to this event in the previous Lectures. To-day it comes to the centre of our attention. It is the event that *God* became *man*, or as John i. 14 puts it more exactly, that the *Word* became *flesh*. Because it concerns nothing more and nothing less than that, this event had to be characterised as of such a nature that it could not be understood from anywhere else, not even from a previous knowledge of man's sin and lost condition, but only out of itself, and could therefore be recognised only in faith's decision. We could also say : the Incarnation of the Word of God is the divine *decision*, which constitutes the content of human faith and which forms it also into a *human* decision : *Dominus noster!*

Now in the part of the symbol that lies before us to-day we have to reckon with a double meaning. That is, the words *conceptus de Spiritu sancto, natus ex Maria virgine* have a general and a special, an inner and an outer, a material and a significative sense. In one way or the other the object to which they point is the event

62

of the *Incarnation*. But that general, inner, material thing of which they speak is the *mystery* itself and as such —that Jesus Christ is true God and true man. And the special, the outer thing, the sign of which they speak is the *miracle*—that Jesus Christ as this true God and man has *God* alone for His Father and therefore the *Virgin* Mary for His mother. The first is the fact of the free grace of God in His revelation. The second is the form and fashion peculiar to His revelation, in which as free grace it gives itself to be known. Let us at once premise : it is sensible and right that in the words of the symbol both of these at once, the one in and with the other, are expressed and set forth : the mystery of the thing *and* the miracle of the sign. No doubt we can and must distinguish here in order to understand. But here we cannot and must not divide. In any case we should consider carefully what we are doing if we are going to separate content from form, the thing from the sign, and then perhaps say " Yes " here, " No " there. Up to now, as far as the eye can reach, the content, the thing, has always been lost when the form, the sign has gone. It is no doubt true that the dogma of the Virgin Birth is only the form and fashion of the witness of the true godhead and manhood of Christ. But it is also true it is just in *this* form and fashion that this witness has been heard by the Church right from the beginning. And it could well be that its clarity and definiteness is inseparably bound up with this form and fashion, that therefore in its clarity and definiteness it is not to be heard otherwise than in this very form and fashion.

But let us direct our attention first of all to this testimony as such, therefore to the general, inner, material sense of our passage. The formula " Conceived by the

Holy Ghost" makes at least this general statement : that the human existence of Jesus Christ in its creature-liness as distinguished from all other creatures, has its origin immediately in God, and is therefore immediately God's own existence. And the formula " Born of the Virgin Mary" makes at least this general statement : that God's own existence in Jesus Christ, without prejudice to the fact that here also God is the Creator, has also a human-creaturely origin and is therefore also human-creaturely existence. What, then, the two formulæ together aim at is not to bring God and man into positions of very great, perhaps infinite nearness, but to say that in the conception and birth of Jesus Christ, God and man became *one*, in order for all time and unto eternity to be one in Him Who was so conceived and born. So that it is as a twofold fact that these two things can be said and must be said of Jesus Christ : He was and is God *and* man ; but always both of them, not one without the other, and both (each in *its own* way !) with equal seriousness and emphasis : neither the one nor the other under reserve, neither the one nor the other in a merely figurative, provisional, metaphorical sense. Jesus Christ is this : not only man, further, not only an exceptional man, further, not only so exceptional a man that we must venture to ascribe to him similarity to or even equality with God, no, but as true *man* so also by origin and in Himself *true* God. Therefore : *conceptus de Spiritus sancto.* And Jesus Christ is this : not only God, and not only one of those lords, angels or demons, one of those powers or ideas, which, together with the heroes of humanity, populate overhead the space between God and man, and which can meet us in men without thereby becoming human reality, no, but

64

as true *God* so also *true* man. Therefore : *natus ex Maria virgine.*

In order to explain what Scripture and Creed testify about this, the point of departure has to be the fact that that Word John i. 14 speaks of a *becoming*, therefore of a history. It is not self-evident, it " is " not simply that God is man. We have already said : here is cause for wonder. And it is just that faith which knows that God is God and man man, that the Creator is not a creature and the Holy One not like one of ourselves that at this point will not cease to wonder. We know of no divine necessity on the basis of which the Word *had* to become flesh. And we have absolutely no knowledge of any human possibility on the basis of which the Word *could* become flesh. We can only know of the actuality : the Word *became* flesh. We can only—and this is the work of faith—seek to *follow* this becoming, to follow this way, this event as such.

We have now to observe further that the event is carried by the ἐγένετο (John i. 14) into the past—a past which is no doubt not a simply concluded past—and is therefore characterised as an objectively *completed* event. What is not self-evident, what we shall never be able to understand is once and for all this : the true God *is* true man in Jesus Christ. Wonder, the wonder of faith, means standing still before that reality in which our legitimate questions as to its divine necessity and its human possibility are set aside. We can no longer put these questions apart from this reality. It can never be the work of faith to go in an arbitrary fashion along a way that is too high for us, but just—to follow. Before we believed, it happened : the Word *became* flesh. In faith we follow this event that preceded our faith.

But it is God Who is the Subject, the Actor in this event. Not man, not God *and* man, but God *alone*. The *Word* became flesh. God's becoming and being man is and remains His *free* decision. The Incarnation means no ascent of man to God, but a descent of God to man. The man Jesus Christ as such has no existence of His own, no abstract existence that could be regarded separately, that could have a separate meaning. The man Jesus Christ has His existence—*conceptus de Spiritu sancto*—directly and exclusively in the existence of the eternal Son of God. What is meant when it is said that the Word became flesh and that Jesus Christ was conceived by the Holy Spirit is that this eternal Son of God took human existence (*Menschsein*) into community of existence (*Gemeinschaft des Existierens*) with Himself. There is nothing said about an intermixing of God and man, or a change of God into a man, or of a man into God, but simply this—that without ceasing to be God, God becomes and is at the same time man. *He* speaks, *He* acts here, He does it as man, but it is *He* Who does it. The power of this Incarnation, the revealing and reconciling power also of His incarnate life are completely *His* power. Faith therefore holds on to the Word, on to the Son of God. How could it hold on to Him if He had not become man ? But how could it hold on to anyone, to anything else in this man than just to the Son of God, Who Himself is this man ?

But the object of divine action in the Incarnation is *man*. God's free decision is and remains a *gracious* decision ; God becomes man, the Word became flesh. The Incarnation means no apparent and reserved, but a real and complete descent of God. God actually became what we are, in order actually to exist *with* us, actually to exist *for* us, in order, in thus becoming and being human, *not* to do what we do—sin ; and to *do* what we fail to do —God's, His own, will ; and so actually, in our place, in our situation and position to be the new man. It is not in His eternal majesty—in which He is and remains hidden from us—but as this new *man* and therefore as the Word in the *flesh*, that God's Son is God's revelation to us and our reconciliation with God. Just for that reason faith cannot look past His humanity, the cradle of Bethlehem and the Cross of Golgotha in order to see Him in His divinity. Faith in the eternal Word of the Father is faith in Jesus of Nazareth or it is not the Christian faith.

We have touched with the greatest brevity on some of the truths that are concentrated in our passage of the symbol and that the Church later attempted to define more clearly and to develop. Here also it did not act in wilful cleverness, but in inevitable conflict with views which were apt to dim or to darken either the *freedom* or the *grace* of the divine decision in Jesus Christ, either the real *divinity* of His manifestation, or the real *revelation* of God that took place in it, and with the one assuredly also the other. If God and man are *not differentiated* in Jesus Christ, then God is not free ; consequently in the manifestation of Jesus Christ, we have not really to do with God's *revelation*. All the deviations here possible have this in common that they call in question the *mystery* of revelation. And on that account the Christology of the early Church concerned itself all along the line with making known and defending the mystery of revelation as such. Its opposition to the heresies which it combated can be generally defined by saying that it summons to *reverence* and to *worship*, while the one-sided views of the Arians and the Docetics, the Mono-physites and the Nestorians are in the last resort to be understood only as coming from dread of reverence and only as invitation to comfortable encounter with an all too near or all too far-off God. The *mystery* of revelation, however, consists simply in the fact that it is, in the genuine Biblical sense of this conception, the *truth*, i.e. the action of the true God towards true man, *free*, because it rests on God's free unmerited compassion, and *gracious*, because in spite of everything and in all reality it comes to meet man. In this unity of freedom and grace, revelation is truth ; but in this very unity, it is also mystery. And this mystery of revelation is the mystery of the true divinity and humanity that are united in the person of Jesus Christ.

We are *shown* that this is so by the second, namely, the special, outer, significative sense of our passage, according to which Jesus Christ, in the just described unity of His being as God and man, was conceived im-mediately by God, namely by the *Holy Spirit* and there-fore was born of the *Virgin* Mary. It has often been asserted that the revelation of God, and therefore the truth, and therefore the mystery, of the unity of God and man in Jesus Christ can be thought of, believed and known and represented perfectly well without this miracle. The brief survey which we have just given seems to confirm that. And so even the orthodox writers on Dogmatics of past ages expressly declared that the unity of the being of Jesus Christ as true God and true man was not substantiated by that miracle and therefore, ᶠor the most part, they spoke of the mystery of the *unio hypostatica* quite separately from the miracle of the *nativitas* of Christ. As a matter of fact, there is no knowing to what extent the doctrine of the Incarnation could not be understood as self-substantiated, or to what extent it should, so far as content is concerned, be in need of supplementing from the doctrine of the Virgin Birth. But it certainly could not be said that the truth and power of the forgiveness of sins pronounced by Jesus (Mk. ii. 5) on the sick of the palsy was based on or increased by His afterwards (Mk. ii. 11) bidding him with such effect take up his bed and go home. Yet this story can manifestly not be read and understood without this miracle of healing. That order to the sick of the palsy is made, according to Mk. ii. 10 : " *That ye may know* that the Son of Man hath power on earth to forgive sins. . . ." This is exactly the relationship also between the mystery of the Incarnation and the miracle of the Virgin Birth. The miracle of the Virgin Birth has not ontic but noetic significance. It advertises what here takes place. As miracle in general, and now as just this special miracle, it is the watch before the door drawing our attention to the fact that we are here concerned with the *mystery*, with *God's free grace*.

I said before that the Christology of the early Church preserves the mystery and therefore summons to reverence and worship. I should like now to add : it does that because it pays heed to this watch at the door. It respects the miracle of the Virgin Birth. It is in and with this respect that it preserves the very knowledge of the Incarnation.

By describing the Incarnation of the Word as the occurrence of a *miracle* the dogma of the Virgin Birth starts off with saying very clearly and impressively : within the continuum of actual human-creaturely history and without eliminating this or even so much as making

69

a rent in it, the Incarnation of the Word is a divine new-beginning ; grace, but grace of the free God ; freedom, but freedom of the gracious God. Therefore there is indeed a unity of God and man ; God Himself *creates* it ; only God *can* create it ; God creates it, because He *wills* to create it. It is no other unity than His own eternal unity as Father and Son. This unity is the Holy Spirit. He and He alone makes the unity of God and man necessary and possible. The Holy Spirit is God Himself in His *freedom* to make His creature fit for communion with Him, capable of receiving Him, object of His revelation. It is through the Holy Spirit that there is in the world that freedom of the Church in which God is heard and proclaimed. The freedom of the children of God in this Church, i.e. the freedom bestowed on men to be children of God, is this freedom of God the Holy Spirit. What the Incarnation is properly and originally concerned with is just this freedom, which is the real basis of the Church, the true birth of all God's children. The flesh, what is human, becomes free to be assumed into that unity with the Son of God only through the Holy Spirit, not through its own capacity. But through the Holy Spirit it really becomes free for that, it really becomes recipient of the eternal Word. That is not to say that the Holy Spirit is the Father of Jesus Christ. The *conceptus de Spiritu sancto* in the symbol, or the New Testament passages to which this statement refers, do not say anything about a marriage between God and a woman. *Conceptus de Spiritu sancto* says rather that, as regards His human existence Jesus Christ has *no* father. It says nothing at all about marriage : it speaks of a creation taking place in Mary. In this miracle that is a pointer to the mystery God's grace is to be seen in the fact that it takes place in

Mary, God's freedom, in the fact that it is creation. Along with the meeting with God and therefore along with the Grace of God, man encounters in this miracle a peculiar judgment. By God's entering as Creator at a point where we expect to hear of the act of marriage of man and wife, manifestly just because the event of revelation affects man in the highest degree, man is in a definite way excluded from co-operation in this event. It is no doubt right to explain this as meaning that *sinful* man is here to be excluded. But the sinful element that has here to be excluded will in that case not have to be sought in the act of marriage or in sexual life as such, but in the sovereignty of human will and power and activity generally and as such. In this sovereignty man is not free for God's Word. He is that, therefore, only when this sovereignty is excluded. He is that, therefore, only when there is excluded that which—be it noted, not arising from Creation, but from the Fall—distinguishes or characterises the *male* as bearer of humanity. Therefore the judgment strikes the male ; therefore Joseph is excluded as earthly father of Jesus. Therefore the object of revelation is woman ; therefore—*ex Maria virgine.* That does not mean any apotheosis of woman. Woman, too, shares in that sovereignty of man, that is excluded by the judgment of grace. Even Mary can only be blessed, because she has believed (Luke i. 45), not on the score of her virginity, not on the score of her femininity. But without desert on her part, she was *chosen* in her femininity, in what makes a relative distinction between her and the male, to be a sign of what, in spite of and in his sin, man can be and do, if and when God concerns Himself with him : " Behold the handmaid of the Lord ; be it unto me according to Thy Word " (Luke i. 38). When his

71

sovereignty is excluded, he is able to believe in the Word of God. It is in this way and in this sense that Mary becomes the mother of the Lord, Who has only an eternal Father.

All this, as *sign* of the Incarnation of the Word, that ye may know that we are here dealing with free grace.— As is well known this dogma has in recent times been much assailed. The exegetical grounds that are usually adduced would not in themselves suffice for its theological criticism. Properly speaking, decisive assault upon it or doubt of it has come only from failure to understand its character as accompanying sign, and therefore from the idea that it might be rejected as an insufficient hypothesis on which to base the Incarnation, or as a superfluous, miraculous embellishment. But it is neither the one nor the other. Again, it advertises what here takes place. Let the answer to such criticism be no more than indicated. Even the negation of the Virgin Birth could advertise something, namely, what happens, or does not happen, in regard to the mystery of revelation in these denying theologies. Is it chance that in the theologians who reject the Virgin Birth one comes, at a lesser or greater remove, upon an " natural theology " limiting the theology of free grace ? *Vestigia terrent.* Most certainly, for reasons that cannot be further elucidated, it might actually be the case, as was indicated at the outset, that it is impossible to separate this content from this form, this form from this content, and that the better course is just to leave this dogma uncriticised.

VIII

PASSUS SUB PONTIO PILATO

IN his Catechism of 1545 Calvin at this passage of the symbol makes the teacher put the following question to the scholar : " Why do you pass immediately from His birth to His death and skip the rest of His life-story ? " Had I been this scholar, I should have answered with the counter-question whether the rest of this life-story of Jesus was actually being skipped. But the answer also, which, according to Calvin's Catechism, the scholar has to give to this question, cannot be described as satisfactory. It runs : " Here (i.e. in the Creed) there is mentioned only what belongs to the real substance of our Redemption." How, we may well ask, could the Church really have been of the opinion, when the symbol came into existence, that Jesus' life-story did not belong to the real substance of our Redemption ? Calvin's living pupils, namely, the authors of the Heidelberg Catechism, saw in this case not only more deeply, but above all more correctly from a Biblical-exegetical point of view than their Master when at the corresponding place (Q. 37) in answer to the question, " What do you understand by the Word, *suffered ?* " they said, " That *all the time He lived on earth, but especially at the end of His life,* He bore, in body and soul, the wrath of God against the sin of the whole human race, in order that by His passion, as the only atoning sacrifice, He might redeem our body and soul from everlasting damnation, and obtain for us the grace of God, righteousness and eternal life ". It is not as if, in contrast to the four Evangelists,

Paul (whose mind Calvin may perhaps have specially intended to give in that question and answer) took less interest or none at all in the rest of Christ's life, in view of the fact that with him we seem to hear only of the death and of the resurrection of Christ. It is rather the case that in speaking of Christ's death Paul was thereby, with somewhat violent abridgment and condensation, speaking of all the rest of His life as well. That this is so may be quite plainly indicated in the passage Phil. ii. 6 f. The best proof of it, however, might be the indirect one, that on closer inspection the four Evangelists themselves have no intention of offering a life-story of Jesus, in which somewhere at the end there is an account also of His death. On the contrary, what they relate of Jesus' first appearance, of His sayings and miraculous acts, of His conversations with His disciples and with His Jewish contemporaries—all that, right from the beginning of all the four Gospels (least perhaps in Luke), converges unmistakably upon that point. It is not only preparation for the story of the Passion, but already it stands under its ever-darkening shadows and, forming with it a complete whole, stands in the light of the Resurrection story which itself stands over against this whole. Even in the passages in Acts (as say, Acts ii. 22 f. ; x. 37 f. ; xiii. 33 f.) in which the nature of apostolic preaching about Jesus is indicated, I cannot find any other relationship that might justify us in speaking of a " filled-out " proclamation (*kerygma*) here and in the Gospels, but of an empty or merely half-filled kerygma in Paul. Just as, in speaking of Christ's death, Paul had in view all the rest of the life of Jesus, so the Evangelists and the Acts of the Apostles, in speaking of this remaining part of the life of Jesus, were looking towards

74

His death. We may assume that our passage in the symbol also is to be explained in this sense. By naming not only the Crucifixion and the death of Jesus Christ, but first and by itself His *Passion*, the symbol clearly does not pass over the remaining life-story of Jesus ; to say the least it points back to " all the time He lived on earth," and characterises it as a whole as a Passiontide.

The Incarnation and therefore the revelation of the Son of God and the reconciliation of the world to God that He effected, means *victory* and triumphal progress, albeit a secret one—yes, very secret, very much hidden. "We beheld His glory" (John i. 14). "He was trans- figured before them, and His face did shine as the sun, and His raiment was white as the light" we read once in the middle of the Gospel story of Jesus' life (Matt. xvii. 2). "Thou art the Christ, the Son of the living God" con- fesses Peter, and it is not flesh and blood, but the heavenly Father of Jesus Christ Who has revealed that to him (Matt. xvi. 16 f.). All miracle stories have in their way, it seems to me, similar significance. They are signs of the coming Kingdom, manifestations of the free grace of God. In the last Lecture we became acquainted in the Virgin Birth with such a sign of the hidden glory of Jesus Christ, and in the narrative of the healing of the sick of the palsy we touched briefly on a second example. But just in this character as *signs* that emerge, but that, far from becoming the rule, disappear again, that, so to say, break into, yes, break through, the life of Jesus in the flesh—all that belongs properly to the *Easter* story. They are rays of His Resurrection and Ascension, pre- cursory, no more than precursory rays that suddenly illuminate quite another field, but then leave it again in darkness. The rule of the life of Jesus in the *flesh* as

75

such is this—that the glory of the eternal Son is *hidden* under the aspect of its opposite.

Jesus *suffers*. Therefore He does not conquer. He does not triumph. He has no success, or such as He has melts away at the crucial moment like snow beneath the sun. It might be easy to explain His passing through all the reaches of our natural life as a sojourner and stranger, His not being related, in any positive way that is discernible, to family, race, state or culture, His not having where to lay His head. But even in that function that is most surely His own, teaching the people, training His disciples, He did not achieve any aims, indeed He does not appear to have so much as striven after any definite aims. The religious leaders of His people treat Him as coldly at the beginning as at the end, as malevolently at the end as at the beginning. With them He achieved nothing except what threatened from the beginning and then in the end came to pass, His crucifixion. The same could be said of His relationship to His people and to His disciples. But even in personality He does not appear to have had anything like so convincing and winning an effect as an amiable Christian journalism and rhetoric have in recent days delighted to represent. Even at the height of His activity He was not spared the cruellest accusations. The populace that to-day shouted " Hallelujah! " will to-morrow cry "Crucify Him! " His disciple, Judas, betrays Him. At last all leave Him, even His favourite disciples, and he upon whom He was to build His Church as upon a rock, Simon Peter, denies Him thrice before the cock crows. And it is just there that His " suffering under Pontius Pilate " properly speaking begins. For long and like a terrifying refrain that ever recurs He kept predicting—and we already have it predicted in Herod's threat to the newborn child, and indeed in the inhospitable environment of His birth—that the Son of Man must suffer many things and be rejected and killed. If there is any aim discernible in this life, any business that it is manifestly engaged in carrying out, it is this : the Son of Man must suffer. He must " be lifted up from the earth " as the essential and final stage of His journey is described in John's Gospel in dreadful ambiguity. The " Passion Story " in the narrower sense, the " suffering under Pontius Pilate " thus really imports nothing that is absolutely new into this life. And so it is not something that could be labelled a catastrophe. It does not take by surprise, it only completes—perhaps one should say : it only brings to the light of day for all to see something that for Jesus Himself had long been a true and present reality. Pontius Pilate the redoubtable, or perhaps not so very redoubtable, procurator of the Roman Emperor, who finds Jesus innocent but yet condemns Him to death, is only the mouthpiece of the world which now says what Jesus Himself said before : the Son of Man must suffer ! For the sake of completeness let us add that even the teaching and instruction that Jesus gives His disciples does not point in any other direction. The future that He sets before their eyes consists in their being persecuted for His name's sake. And what He demands of them is that they take up their cross. " If they have called the master of the house Beelzebub, how much more shall they call them of His household ? " (Matt. x. 25). Consolation, help and hope will not be wanting there, as surely as the suffering of Jesus Himself is not without this limit : " on the third day He will rise again ". But—that is the limit, that stands in another book.

If we keep to the first book, to the question : What is the meaning of the revelation of God in the flesh, of the human existence of Jesus ? then the answer must run : In contrast to what revelation seems to mean, it means *concealment* of God. It does not mean light but darkness. It does not mean an overcoming of the world, its liberation from sin, from evil, from death, from the devil. On the contrary it means humiliation and surrender of the Son of God to all those powers of impossibility, of atheism. It means not His victory, but theirs. It does not mean the annulment of God's wrath, or even its lessening or lightening ; it means simply, as we heard the Catechism put it, the bearing of " the wrath of God against the whole human race ". It means the " suffering under Pontius Pilate ". It is no doubt true that this suffering has, as we have just said, a frontier and therefore a meaning and a future. Indeed, we heard what follows : " . . . in order that by His passion, as the only atoning sacrifice, He might redeem our body and soul from everlasting damnation, and obtain for us the grace of God, righteousness and eternal life ". But this already expresses what is to be said of Good Friday when we look back at it from Easter. On Good Friday itself—and not only on Good Friday but " all the time He lived on earth "—the suffering of Jesus, just because it is the suffering of God's wrath against the whole human race, has no frontier, no meaning, no future. How could He who actually places Himself where the whole human race stands, namely, under the wrath of God—and Jesus *did* place Himself there !—how could He see a frontier, a meaning and a future in what He had there to suffer ? The abyss into which sin hurls us, yes us, is just this, that we do not know how deep this abyss actually is, this suffering *without* frontiers, *without* meaning and

78

without future. This burden can only be borne. And Jesus bears it. His Incarnation means *that*. " All flesh is as grass, and all the goodliness thereof is as the flower of the field : the grass withereth, the flower fadeth : because the spirit of the Lord bloweth upon it : surely the people is grass " (Is. xl. 6 f.). And the Word, the Word of God, became flesh, became therefore just what this people is. As comrade of that people, as true man, Jesus bears this burden : because " the justice of God requires that the same human nature which has sinned should make satisfaction for sin " (Heidelberg Catechism, Q. 16).

In view of this riddle it is not wise to open at once that other book that contains its solution, but first of all to let it stand as a riddle and say what it has to say. The book of the victory of God and of our redemption can only be read when the book of the suffering of Jesus Christ has been read to the end. In the next Lecture when we shall be occupied with the *crucifixus, mortuus sepultus* we shall read it to the end with the horror that befits this subject.

We shall linger to-day for a little over the very remarkable point that the suffering of Jesus is named His " suffering *under Pontius Pilate*". How does Pontius Pilate get into the Credo ? The simple answer can at once be given : it is a matter of date. The name of the Roman procurator in whose term of office Jesus Christ was crucified, proclaims : at such and such a point of *historical time* this happened. And the symbol intends to express just that : that what it has to say about Jesus Christ happened at a definite and definitely assignable time within that time which is ours also. With that a line is drawn, a polemic is directed against a Gnostic Christ-idealism. If the Word became flesh, then it

79

became temporal, and the reality of the revelation in Jesus Christ was what we call the lifetime of a man. It was not only that, but it was also that. It is an eternal but no timeless reality ; it is at once an eternal and a temporal reality. It is not a timeless essence of all or of some times. It is not to be discovered by laboriously extracting such a thing as a timeless spirit or a timeless substance out of all times or out of definite times, even that of the years 1 to 30. It will never be understood by anyone who is irritated by its concretion, who would like to free it of the temporal that clings to it, who fancied that he could get past its temporal concretion to its ideal substance. It is essentially concrete and therefore temporal and therefore capable of temporal definition, in the same way as, say, the rule of Pericles in Athens. The man who is hankering after the so-called " eternal verities " had best, if he is determined not to be converted, leave his faith uncontaminated with Christian faith. Revelation is a *hic et nunc,* once and for all and unique, or it is not the revelation to which Holy Scripture bears witness. Therefore, *sub Pontio Pilato.* The man has his rightful place in the Credo. If only it had always been borne in mind that he really stands in the Credo ! Then the Church and Theology would have been spared many false and crooked by-paths.

But now it may well be asked why it is to a profession of faith in a *suffering* Christ that this date is attached. Why not to His birth ? Why do we not hear the name of the governor Cyrenius, known from Luke ii. 2, in connection with the *natus ex virgine ?* I do not think that that is chance or caprice. On the contrary, I think that here we have cropping up for the first time a hint which will be fully unfolded at the end of the second

80

article of the Creed where Christ's Ascension, Session at the Right Hand of God, and Second Coming are dealt with. This time which is reckoned by the names of the Roman procurators or even Roman Emperors or in any such way, this historical time, is, in its entirety, including its most distant past and future, the time of the man of disobedience and anarchy. It was into this historical time that Christ was born in order to exist in it, in the years 1 to 30 of this time, as in our time—how would He be man if it were otherwise ? As the time of the man of disobedience and disorder it is the time which still continues by the patience of God but which—under God's wrath—can only continue as a time destined to *pass away* and quickly passing. The fashion of this world—and that will mean *time*—passeth away (1 Cor. vii. 31). For this reason it is the time—and now we understand the inner connection between *passus* and *sub Pontio Pilato*—in which the Son of God as true Son of Man must *suffer*, the time in which He must have everything *against* Him, success and fortune, wicked men and good, State and Church, His own human nature —which is indeed " flesh "—yes, and God Himself. It is the time in which He must bear the burden of the *wrath* of God. What can he be here but the absolute stranger ? What can He do here but by His very existence occasion scandal ? What form can He have here but the " form of a servant " (Phil. ii. 7) entirely without beauty : " He is despised and rejected of men, a man of sorrows, and acquainted with grief ; and we hid as it were our faces from Him ; He was despised, and we esteemed Him not " (Is. liii. 3) ? If the Word became flesh and therefore temporal, and if the time was *this* time, our *world*-time, the time that is dated by Pontius

Pilate and his like, while for a hero or half-God this time could and can still be a great and beautiful time (God's patience extends even to heroes and half-gods !), for the eternal Son of the Father it could be nothing else than passion-time. The Son of God Who has become temporal, Who has entered world-time, could, as a child, only lie in the manger and as a man only die on the Cross. World-time had nothing else, this age by the mouth of Pontius Pilate had nothing else to say to Him than sentence of death, not in spite of His innocence, but because of it, because He was the only Innocent One in this age. But what else could the death-sentence from the mouth of Pilate be but at the same time the death-sentence of this age ? What does it signify for this world-time that the eternal Son of God can only suffer in it, can only die in it ? Is it He or is it not rather world-time that is judged ? Are His " sufferings under Pontius Pilate " not already the birth-pangs of a new time, which will be not world-time, but God's time, the time of the new man, and therefore the time of free grace for the human race rescued from the old world-time that passes away ? With this suffering that signifies this judgment are we not already, while we are in the middle of the first book, being pointed to the other, the second book ? Well, we could not say all that, even in this interrogatory fashion, if we had not already looked across from this strange *sub Pontio Pilato* into that other book from which we know that it is by no self-deception that we see in the very *humiliation* of God, in His revelation—not in spite of its being humiliation, but because of it—secret but supremest *victory* and *triumph*. And indeed it cannot be otherwise if it is really true *God* Who has abased Himself and become true man.

IX

CRUCIFIXUS, MORTUUS ET SEPULTUS, DESCENDIT AD INFEROS

HAVING characterised the second Article as the centre of the whole Creed, we shall have to call the clauses that deal with the *death* and the *resurrection* of Jesus Christ the centre within this centre. The work of New Testament exegesis shows no clearer result than this : that from all sides the witness of the Apostles and Evangelists pours in upon this centre : *crucifixus est et resurrexit.* Here all the threads of Christian knowledge run together visibly or invisibly. It is from here that the significance for the Christian Credo of the Incarnation, of the Second Coming, and even of Creation or of the Church is to be gauged. It is here, therefore, that the spirits are separated. It is here that the Credo is understood or not understood. It is here that it is dead recitation in a Church that does not know that, what it thinks it has, must be not only kept, but also acquired. Or, on the other hand, it is here that it is the Confession of a Church that believes, and that therefore knows both what it believes, and what it ventures to say in its belief. It is here that in the very thing that the Credo wants to say with the greatest urgency, it is frustrated by theologians and preachers or by their readers and hearers or by both— like people, so to say, who have stolen something and would like to avoid returning to the scene of their crime. But it is here also that it has its power in the Church, in the preaching, in the theology that really allow themselves to be rallied and directed by this, its most urgent call; and no less in the life of the individual believers who let themselves be upheld and moved by this call in toil, in suffering, in temptation, and in the very hour of death. It is just here that the Object of the Creed enters into inevitable judgment against *all* human knowing and confessing, yes, against *all* the attitudes and responsibilities that man assumes towards Him, no matter how well they may be meant, how earnestly and piously carried out. Yet it is just here that men should practise committing confidently to the compassion of God their whole knowing and confessing, their whole human relationship with the Object of the Creed, i.e. with God, in other words, should practise really holding on to the righteousness of *faith* and not at all to the righteousness of their theological, ecclesiastical, pious or moral *works*.

We begin our consideration of the doctrine of the *death* of Jesus Christ with a glance at the humblest part of our symbol; I mean the word *sepultus*. This truth that is in itself so trivial, so insignificant, so little likely to give any information, the truth that Jesus Christ was buried, was to Paul, as is to be learned from 1 Cor. xv. 4, a matter of moment. Strange to say, he perceived in it the reality of what is met with in *baptism :* that we are buried with Christ (Rom. vi. 4; Col. ii. 12). First of all the mention in the symbol of the *burial* of Jesus Christ has evidently a function quite similar to the previous mention of Pontius Pilate: it is another reminder of the true *humanity* of Christ. It is a more fundamental and comprehensive reminder of that than

84

the *sub Pontio Pilato.* To say that He was buried is the most unambiguous way in which it is possible to stamp a being as a true actual man. An angel or an idea or the " essence of Christianity " obviously cannot be buried. But Jesus Christ was buried. So, and this is the remarkable thing, there is a point, namely, this point in the Credo, where the word of the believer completely coincides with the word of the unbeliever. *Sepultus* is something that besides the Church Fathers and Luther and Calvin, also Celsus, also Voltaire, also D. Fr. Strauss could say. Assuredly what they were saying on the two sides were quite different things. But they had to say them with the self-same word. This is a fact calculated to lend interest to the *sepultus* which immediately precedes the *resurrexit.* In its very triviality it has evidently an extremely critical significance. By a man's being buried it is evidently confirmed and sealed—seemingly in his presence, actually already in his absence—that he has no longer a present any more than a future. He has become, if I may put it so, pure *past.* He is accessible only to memory, and even that only so long as those who are able and willing to remember him are not themselves buried. And the future towards which all human present is running is just this : to be buried. If *Sepultus est* is said of anyone in retrospect, that is the strongest possible way of saying, He was a true real man. Since the end is burial, to be human means, to run towards pure past. In *this* sense *Jesus Christ,* too, became *man.* Christian faith confesses it, but just here even unbelief will not refuse to follow. The more it is really unbelief, the more energetically, unreservedly and bluntly it, too, will here assert : *Jesus Christus sepultus est.*

Yet we are not dealing here with an *analogia entis*, with a point of attachment, with a common basis for a dialogue between faith and unbelief. It is not possible for unbelief to say *sepultus est* so energetically, so unreservedly, so bluntly, that what faith has to say with the same word can be glimpsed even from afar. For that it would itself have to be faith. No doubt as unbelief it can attempt more or less radically and consistently to explain, to exegise what it means to be man and therefore to run towards pure past. But no explanation of this reality will bring him so much as one step nearer to what is asserted of Jesus Christ as the subject of this clause : *sepultus est.* For with this clause there is thus asserted : once it happened that it was confirmed and sealed that in and with this man, Jesus of Nazareth, God Himself had not only no future but no present and therefore became pure past. If unbelief were to repeat this clause so interpreted, that is, interpreted in the sense of the symbol, it would manifestly have to be not unbelief but *faith in God*, and at that, not faith in any God in general but faith in God in Christ and therefore in God's *revelation.* The analogy between the utterance of faith and the utterance of unbelief crops up only immediately to disappear again. It is not possible to lay hold of it and to discuss it as a common text between different interpretations of which a choice could be made. The choice here is not between two interpretations, but between faith and unbelief. And the choice has already *been* made between the two when both make the same statement : *Jesus Christus sepultus est.*

In the context of the Christian Creed this statement declares (and this is the very thing that made it important to Paul), that the way of God into humiliation, entered upon in the Incarnation of the Word and trodden in the passion of the Son of God within this our world-time, was continued into the very deepest, most ultimate *concealment of His divine existence.* The deepest most ultimate meaning of " He made Himself of no reputation and took upon Him the form of a servant " (Phil. ii. 8) is expressed by the *sepultus.* It means that God veiled His eternity, and in becoming temporal in His human existence in Jesus Christ, accepted also this : His becoming in this, His human existence, what every man becomes, pure past. Therefore what gives the *sepultus est* its place in the Christian creed is decidedly, that it speaks of an act of God and indeed—it can scarcely be expressed otherwise—of a *self-surrender of God to the state and fate of man,* a self-surrender in which He does not cease to be God, but yet makes the state and fate of man His own in such a way that His *divine existence* for all other eyes than His own becomes absolutely *invisible. Paulisper interea delitescebat eius divinitas, hoc est vim suam non exserebat* (Calvin). No man knows the Son save the Father. For to whom else should God's divine being be visible at the place where He is buried as man and therefore becomes pure past ?

But with this self-surrender of God to the state and fate of man, which we find represented with devastating finality in the *sepultus* of the Christian Credo, there now falls on this very state and fate of man a light which we cannot obtain as the result of any anthropological analysis but can only accept as knowledge offered to us in God's revelation. This brings us to the proper Good Friday message, to the consideration of which we now address ourselves in the other clauses of this section.

The words *crucifixus*, *mortuus*, *descendit ad inferos* have, generally speaking, a double aspect.

1. They describe what befalls the man Jesus of Nazareth as the bearing of a divine *curse* (that is what *crucifixus* means according to Gal. iii. 13), as the endurance of a divine *punishment* (that is what *mortuus* means, if according to Rom. vi. 23 the wages of sin is death), as the misery of an *ordeal* allowed by God (which is what *descendit ad inferos* means, if Calvin has understood it rightly in referring it to Mark xv. 34 : " My God, My God, why hast Thou forsaken Me ? "). Now certainly that is a very remarkable and extraordinary description of the death of Jesus of Nazareth. We understand it when, and only when, we keep before our eyes what has just been said, that what is involved in the life and, crowning all, in the death of Jesus of Nazareth is the self-surrender of *God* to the state and fate of man. What is confirmed and sealed by the burial of a man—namely, that he has now become pure past—is not itself bound up with the conceptions, curse, punishment and ordeal. The death of a man, and even the violent and painful death of an innocent, yes, good man, will be experienced by him and will inevitably be conceived by others as something completely, absolutely different from curse, punishment and ordeal. Who of us would at any death-bed—and even in thinking of what happened at Golgotha—ever stumble upon this thought ? It is in truth a thought upon which we cannot come. But as God's thought it has come to us, since at Golgotha not only an innocent, nay, a good man died a violent and painful death, but since there in the form of a criminal's death and as confirmation and seal, in the form of the *sepultus est*, the eternal God Himself

88

made our state and fate His own. When this man passes away in death, death that we accept dully or only a little moved when we see it in others, and that we ourselves go to meet just as dully or only a little disturbed, when we see it in Him, what can we know of anything in it that makes it more than just another of those riddles of our existence which we can bear very well by facing up to them with optimistic or pessimistic thoughts, thoughts that are all too knowing or all too sceptical ? Is there any one of us who has been condemned to a sleepless night by the knowledge : I shall one day be buried and then be " pure past " ? This conception in the form in which we have fashioned it and tricked it out with our own ideas is poles away from what the Creed says in *crucifixus, mortuus, descendit ad inferos*. Actually we know nothing of the fact that the inevitable future which burial holds for man means curse, punishment and ordeal above all ordeal : dereliction by God of one sentenced and chastised by God ! We know nothing about man's being rightfully and therefore of necessity *killed* by God. *We cannot* know of it. We could not even for a moment bear to know of it. But Jesus Christ *did* know of it. He could know of it and He could bear to know of it ; what He did bear on Golgotha, He could bear as curse, punishment and ordeal because He was man like us, but yet as man like us God Himself. The self-surrender of God to our state and fate is required that it may gain this frightful meaning and content of a suffering of divine wrath. The eternal Word has got to be present in our flesh, that, as it is put in Rom. viii. 3, " sin may be condemned in the flesh," i.e. that man in all that he is and does may as sinner be placed openly and simultaneously

89

in judgment, i.e. under the sentence and punishment of God, and that he may now experience what it means to have forsaken God and therefore in turn to be forsaken by God. The presence of God, and only that, makes the cross the Cross, that is the cursed tree ; makes death punishment, that is, righteous and irrevocable retribution ; makes the inconceivable way that is to be trodden in death the descent into hell, i.e. the sinking into that despair : "My God, my God, why hast Thou forsaken Me ? " He, God, makes Him "Who knew no sin" "to be sin" (ἁμαρτίαν ἐποίησεν, 2 Cor. v. 21), that is, to be one over whom breaks curse, punishment and ordeal. If God had not become man in Jesus Christ, had not descended to that deepest ultimate concealment of His divinity, in truth we neither could nor would know what sin is and therefore what judgment is. In Jesus Christ it meets us as condemned sin. *Ecce homo :* *there, that* is man : the enemy of God and therefore— for who could hope to resist God ?—crushed by the wrath of God. We may, we must now after the event, listen to Christ's telling us who we are ourselves, what is our significance and fate that God has there made His own, telling us what is in truth the importance of the burial, of the passing away that we have all to face. It is something that even now we have got to be *told*. Even now we do not ourselves become Christ. It would be a more than Promethean faith to want to experience as our own a repetition of His suffering, His cross, His death, His descent into hell. Let us—we shall have enough to do with that—have what we are, brought *in Him* to the light of God. Let it be that *He* has encountered all that would bring upon us curse, punishment, ordeal. It is enough to let this be true and valid for us—namely, that we *are* sinners : that our sin *has been* condemned. If that holds good as revealed *in Him* and executed *on Him*, then the humiliation and discipline prescribed for us and supportable by us will not be lacking. But the sufferings of Christ are not prescribed for us and besides they would not be supportable by us. " He who sees God, dies." Even Christ died as man, since He saw God. And it was only because He Himself was God that the resurrection could and had to follow this death.

2. But now the same words *crucifixus, mortuus, descendit ad inferos* describe what befell the man Jesus of Nazareth as at once the execution of an *acquittal* that is passed upon us (*crucifixus* signifies : " He hath blotted out the handwriting that was against us . . . and hath taken it out of the way, nailing it to the cross," Col. ii. 14), as the making of a *sacrifice* offered on our behalf (*mortuus* means : " He gives His life a ransom for many," Mark x. 45), as the occurrence of a divine *victory* creating space and air (*descendit ad inferos* means : " He preached unto the spirits in prison," I Pet. iii. 19, and " the lion of the tribe of Judah hath prevailed," Rev. v. 5). Again it must be said at the outset that this characterisation of the death of Jesus of Nazareth is anything but obvious, and that we can understand it only when we keep before our eyes the fact that when the New Testament and the Creed speak of the life and death of this man, they are thinking directly of the self-surrender of *God* that took place in this life and death. In itself, indeed, the death of a man, as confirmed and sealed by his burial, is still less to be understood as acquittal, sacrifice and victory than above as judgment. The objective brutality of the occurrence that finds its conclusion in a man's burial

would have to be overlooked in a remarkable way, if
there were to be induced here the subjective feeling :
that in certain cases the death of others or even one's
own may appear as something in the nature of a redemption, or if reflections were to be induced by means of
which it could be explained as a death " for " others.
In objective reality no one is happy at the thought that
he must die, and no brother is able to redeem another.
All such thoughts are at best, that is when they are not
self-deception and trifling, reflection of a thought upon
which we could not come of ourselves but which has
come to us afresh as thought of God, since Jesus Christ
the eternal God Himself made our state and fate His
own. We certainly know nothing of the fact that the
passing of man in death is curse, punishment and ordeal.
We know it only as one of the riddles of our existence.
But other than as one of these *riddles* it is not in actual
fact known to us. We have absolutely no knowledge
of its solution. We do not know of any *positive* significance of the fact that the whole of our existence with
its ups and downs, its comings and goings, ends in a
grave. With regard to others, and, though it is harder,
even with regard to ourselves, we can come to terms
with it, and we actually do come to terms with it. But
we can in no wise overcome the disquietude that in death
we have in every case to do with a passing away, that is,
with an unparalleled loss and end. We cannot raise
ourselves above the wall that stands in front of us in
this passing, and therefore we cannot in actual fact get
over it even in our thinking. Again the self-surrender
of God is required in order that here, too, a *divine quickening* take place, in order that here it can be said : acquittal,
sacrifice, victory. The presence of the eternal Word in

our flesh is required, in order that at this place may be heard not only that riddle with which we do indeed come to terms, without being able to get the better of it, but in order that at this place what becomes manifest in the very presence of the eternal Word as *judgment*, may the more exhibit itself as *grace*, the curse therefore as acquittal, the punishment as sacrifice, the ordeal as victory. If these ideas had been thought out and uttered by us, they would be irresponsible, foolish and vain paradoxes. But what ought we and what are we to say if in Jesus Christ it is as these apparent paradoxes assert, and that, in actual fact, for this very reason, that the unity of God and man in Him cannot be *judgment* more profoundly and strongly than it is now really *grace*, in and with and in spite of the judgment, grace, that is, reconciliation of man to God ? If God Himself in Jesus Christ bears the *curse* that must fall upon the transgressors of His law, then it really *is* borne ; then there can be no thought of our bearing it again and further. Then we are acquitted according to the law, yes, declared righteous. For if God's curse no longer falls on us, what can we be —there is no third possibility—what can we be in His sight, and that means in reality, but righteous ? If God Himself in Jesus Christ suffers the *punishment* that our existence would have to incur, then that means that He, this Other, has sacrificed His existence for us. It follows that we can only recognise ourselves as those whom He has thereby won for Himself, who have therefore become His property. If God will not punish us because the punishment is over and done with, then that means that we may now live as those who have been released by Him and who are therefore His own. Finally, if, without ceasing to be God, God in Jesus

93

Christ entered into the ordeal, if Jesus Christ descended into hell and thereby actually doubted Himself as to His being God and man in one, what else can we take that to mean than that He did that also for us and so relieved us of it ? It is no longer *necessary* that we go to hell. And we shall no longer require to go to hell in order to ask ourselves there : why has God forsaken us ? If we think we have occasion for this question, we should consider that Jesus Christ put it long ago and answered it in our place. How could His way into hell have been other than a victorious way ? And by this victorious way He has made a breathing space for us, i.e. the peace that garrisons our hearts and minds, that is and continues to be peace in face of every ordeal because, passing all understanding, it is His own peace, the peace of God.

From this point we can look back again to the remarkable fact that Paul saw the reality of what happens to man in *baptism* in this : that we are buried with Christ. It is actually possible for that which is the burial of Christ to be present now to us. It is the decisive word of that free grace in which in Jesus Christ God gave up His own Son for us. Burial *with* Christ would then mean, we were standing under His *Name* as actually those for whom that took place, who now may *live* as those for whom it did take place.

X

TERTIA DIE RESURREXIT A MORTUIS

IN their context in the Christian Creed the words *crucifixus, mortuus et sepultus, descendit ad inferos* are the very opposite of a cry of despair that would be overpowered and pass into jubilation only with the *resurrexit*. Art may be given the licence—in any case it has often enough made use of it in word and picture and melody—to represent the matter in this dramatic way. But Christian doctrine and preaching must not allow this to confuse them in their knowledge that the word of the Cross is understood and delivered in the sense of Scripture and the Creed, namely, as " power of God " (1 Cor. i. 18) only where it proclaims in all its awful gravity the joy and the peace of the Easter message, just as on the other hand the *resurrexit* does not eliminate the whole misery and interrogation of Good Friday but includes them in itself in such a way that it is only by looking out from it that they can be regarded really as misery and interrogation. The Crucified is the *Risen One* and the Risen One is the *Crucified*.

The resurrection of Jesus Christ is, it is true, a separate event, different from His death, following it in time. The intention of that Gnostic version of the New Testament witness, according to which Christ was immediately awakened from the dead on the Cross and went towards heaven, is easily understood : These two events had evidently to be brought together into simultaneity. But the genuine New Testament witness separates them by speaking emphatically of the *three days*, and thereby qualifies the forty days that follow these three days as a time differentiated from the time between the birth and the death of Jesus. We already spoke of the fact that even in the preceding time this second, new time made itself known. I recall here particularly the story of the transfiguration on the mount which can scarcely be interpreted otherwise than as a piece of anticipated resurrection history. Again I mention the " signs ". They warn us against separating these two times abstractedly. The whole *life and death* of Jesus are undoubtedly interpreted in the light of His *resurrection*, just as on the other hand even the New Testament resurrection stories unmistakably remind us in their details of the *continuity* of this second and that first time.

There is, however, an inner necessity for the distinction of the two. For while that first period from the birth to the death of Jesus brings before our eyes the Incarnation of the Word in Him, God's revealing and reconciling work, yet it brings it before our eyes definitely in its necessary *disguise*, definitely in the form of the *suffering* Jesus, definitely therefore as the humiliation of the eternal Son of God bound up with the self-surrender of God to our human state and fate. God's work here (if we disregard the " signs ") in its disguise, demands *faith ;* it cannot be seen. And so the attitude towards Jesus not only of the people, but also of the disciples is here one that is uncertain, ambiguous, regularly described as " little faith," something halfway between understanding and the complete lack of it, between obedience and disobedience. But what finally appears—we think again of the treachery of Judas, the denial of Peter, the flight of the disciples—is incomprehension and disobedience. Objective, too, is the last thing that remains to be mentioned here, the burial. Here the disguise is complete. Regarded from the conditions of this first period faith and faith alone will penetrate it. And there, too, the matter will end. Christian faith will ever be faith in the Word of the God *concealed* in the form of the suffering Christ, yes of *Christ sepultus* ; and it will therefore ever be a step into utter *darkness*. It were not faith, were it not to lay hold on Him Whom it does not see, as though it saw Him.

Yet even this *faith* is not *thrown upon its own resources*. One has to be very careful in describing faith as a " venture ". That it certainly is. But it is not an intuition or hypothesis hazarded and carried through in any kind of human daring. In being a human venture it is a divine *gift*. Without any effort, emotion or rapture it rests upon a foundation laid with the utmost objectivity. It positively lives by God's revelation. And it can live by it, it can be something more than " little faith " because God's revelation is not only disguise, but also disclosure of the Word of God, not only revelation of the Father through the Son but also revelation of the Son through the Father. And that now is the meaning of Easter Day, the meaning of the second period which, according to the witness of the New Testament, followed that first period. The significance of this day and this period cannot be too comprehensively understood and represented. Not simply the life and death of Jesus of Nazareth as such, not simply the years 1 to 30, but strictly speaking the time of revelation is the forty days after Easter. The content of *that time* is the content of memory, which thereupon became the content of the apostolic witness. Granted that the memory of the first period becomes the content of the apostolic witness, it is that because and in so far as it is illuminated by the memory of this second period. To be a witness of Jesus Christ (Acts i. 8) means in all circumstances to be a " witness of His resurrection" (Acts i. 22). It was not through his having known Christ " after the flesh " (2 Cor. v. 16) that Paul also became an apostle, but through the risen Christ's appearing to him too, in other words, because in his own phrase as " one born out of due time," he was drawn belatedly into the history of the forty days (1 Cor. xv. 8). Since revelation as disclosure, the revelation of the Son through the Father, is according to the New Testament a *second period after* that first one, and itself like that first one *history*, that is, resurrection history, since that is so the message of Jesus Christ is on this side, too, distinguished from an arbitrary *interpretation* of history. That means that Christian faith is not to be understood as idealism that has succeeded in discovering light in darkness, life in death, the majesty of God in the lowliness of human existence and destiny. On the contrary *that* light, *that* life, *that* God are acknowledged by Him Himself Who without any human aid and against all human expectation, as light broke through the darkness, as life overcame death, as God triumphed in and over the lowliness of human existence and destiny. *Resurrexit* means —*Jesus* is conqueror. A Christian Easter sermon had best be silent over the longings and outpourings of human optimism. Christian faith is happy and confident because and in virtue of this fact, that in the very exaltation of Jesus Christ, not faith, but, just as in His humiliation, Jesus Christ Himself acted, that is, *God* in Christ ; happy and confident that the very disclosure of God in His revelation is not interpretation of history but, equally with His concealment, *is history*. We may here recall again the answer given in the first period to the confession of Peter : " Blessed art thou, Simon Bar-jona : for flesh and blood hath not revealed it unto thee, but my Father which is in heaven " (Matt. xvi. 17). Therefore it is with emphasis, meaning exactly what the words say, that faith confesses : *tertia die resurrexit a mortuis*.

If we want to understand the content of that second and peculiar period of the revelation in Jesus Christ characterised by these words, probably our best course is to use here also the two conceptions that forced themselves upon us in our discussion of the Incarnation : the conception of the *matter* or *thing*, and the conception of the *sign*, or concretely stated : the conception of the secret, and the conception of the miracle.

This time we begin with miracle, since what Scripture and Creed tell us about the exaltation of Jesus Christ that followed His humiliation, about this second and peculiar period of His revelation, shows itself at once and at the first glance as miracle. The content of the New Testament Easter story is a single miracle. We say the same when we say : it is a single sign. That which in the preceding history of the life and death of Jesus was a no doubt frequent exception, here becomes the rule. Almost without interruption—except for short scenes where we find the " terrified " disciples by themselves—we have here to do with an occurrence which, while it takes place also in space and time, in Jerusalem and Galilee and still *sub Pontio Pilato*, therefore in the continuum of the history of our world, is yet conceivable by us as actual occurrence only on the one pre-supposition : that *God* as Creator and

99

Lord of this our world, and therefore in free control of what we regard as the regular course of events in this world, is *directly* the *subject* of this occurrence. The miracle consists in the two facts that belong together and that, at least in the opinion of all the New Testament witnesses, are not explicable on the assumption of fraud or deception or by the possibility of a mere vision—the one, that the *grave* of that Jesus who died on the Cross on Good Friday was found *empty* on the third day, the other that Jesus Himself " appears," as the characteristic expression puts it, to His disciples as visibly, audibly, tangibly alive. The concrete content of the memory of the forty days is : Christ is risen, He is risen indeed ! To be exegetically accurate we must understand by this " indeed " corporeally risen ; and thus, if we are not to make so bold as to substitute for the apostolic witness another one altogether, there cannot be any talk of striking out the empty grave. It is of course a notorious fact that the tradition that we have received of this memory of the forty days is in its details in remarkable disorder, far from satisfactory to the historian. But alongside of that stands the other fact that, in spite of very pressing apologetic needs and although that disorder could not even then be concealed from anyone, this tradition was unconcernedly taken up into the New Testament in this very condition. This indicates that there have at any rate been times when no surprise was felt at the witness of apostles and evangelists seeming (just at this central spot) to fall into a stammering, into contradictions as if from the effect of an earthquake. That will occasion no astonishment when the object of this witness is known. Of course it is possible, indeed necessary, to be astonished —even when the state of the tradition is, in view of what was to be handed down, not found to be inexplicable—to be astonished at what remains over (after all obscurities and contradictions have been reckoned with), as the unanimous expression of all the witnesses : at the very miracle of the resurrection. In relation to it, as in the case of the Virgin Birth, every explanation breaks down, because every explanation would have to dissolve the very thing that is to be explained. On the assumption that it was so on that third day and as (allowing for all the historical uncertainties in the forty days that followed) the whole New Testament witnesses, we can only make this remark not by way of proof but of explanation : *if* the *sepultus est* was the last word of the first " non-miraculous " period of revelation, and *if* we have rightly understood this *sepultus est* as the completed self-surrender of God to the human state and fate as to something that is passing away, then the continuation of this history *could* only be the dawn of a new time. In other words, it could only be an occurrence in which the self-surrender of God to the human state and fate really reached completion, that is, became manifest as God's *sovereignty* over this state and fate. Therefore it could only be an occurrence to which God as its subject, unperturbed by the course which it had to take according to the laws which we know regulate everything that happens, gave that turn, which was the only one possible where He was subject. *In concreto* it had to consist in God's *holding up* and putting a stop to the inevitable destiny to *pass away* and be no more, which attaches to the human existence He accepted and assumed, and had accordingly to consist in His raising Jesus from the dead. When, therefore, we have confessed in faith, *sepultus est*, then we are able—not to draw a logical conclusion ! it does not lie in our power to do that—but, following the course which the matter itself makes inevitable, again to confess in faith : *tertia die resurrexit a mortuis.* From a *sepultus est* uttered in unbelief we shall naturally never be able to advance to the *resurrexit.* If the miracle of the resurrection is the sign of that divine way, then there is no denying that as miracle it has its place, its good and necessary place, and further, that not in spite of but just *because* of its being a miracle and indeed *this* miracle, it cannot be repudiated by a faith that follows the divine way, but on the contrary can only be thankfully affirmed.

The *secret* of Easter, on which something must be said in conclusion, can in its substance be none other than that of Good Friday—which again is that of Christmas. There is only *one* secret of Christian faith : God and man in their community through God's free grace. What in particular makes, in this instance, this one secret the mystery of Easter is, to put it in the simplest way, this : that all that we have recognised as the mystery of Good Friday is, as God's decree, will and deed, *true* and *valid.* At the beginning we said one cannot believe in the Cross of Christ otherwise, and one cannot understand the Cross otherwise, than from His resurrection. All that in the crucifixion of Christ was done by God in a hidden way is by the resurrection set in the *light* and put into *force.* If what happened there is not hidden from us, then that is because Christ is risen. Because Christ is risen, and that is, because God goes His way in the Incarnation of His Word right to the *end* and because this end of His way means a *new beginning* for this flesh, i.e. for the human existence and destiny that God made His own in Jesus Christ. If this new beginning is *manifest* to us, then the significance also of the beginning of that way right up to the *sepultus* is by no means hidden. It means that what there befalls human state and fate, curse, punishment and ordeal, is a *divine killing*, but that, with what happened there, there was also carried out a *divine quickening*: an acquittal, a redeeming sacrifice, a victory for man. The new beginning, the resurrection of Jesus Christ, has nothing to add to that. The resurrection only *reveals* it, reveals that this is the way God has actually gone in the concealment of His surrendered, humiliated and suffering Son. The resurrection reveals it, in other words, says to us that this is true and therefore true *for us*, that it is *for us* that God has gone this way in His Son. It is no bold surmise, no dialectic sophistry, no religious arrogance if we believe—believe in face of sin, evil, death and devil—that God's wrath does not fall upon us, that we are righteous, that we are free, that is, that we are God's and that the peace that passeth all understanding may be our consolation. In all that we are arrogating nothing to ourselves. Not for a moment do we forget that our whole being and all our thoughts, words and works are liable to utter damnation. But we ask : " Who is he that shall condemn ? It is Christ that died, yea rather, That is risen again " (Rom. viii. 34). It is because He is risen again, because the self-surrender of God completed itself in the dawn of a new time, because the dawn of this new time was proclaimed to us, and because we can no more forget it, it is on that account that we put that question so defiantly. With that question we are merely allowing God to be God ! In allowing God to be God, the God Who in Christ went this way, in giving Him His place in faith as the God Who in Christ has killed us, too, and made us alive, we are new men " begotten again unto a lively hope by the resurrection of Jesus Christ from the dead "

(1 Pet. i. 3).   It is *free* grace that is the mystery of Easter. For most certainly in going thus to the end of His way God has shown Himself as the free Lord over human existence and destiny.   Most certainly this could bring Him no qualification to make such an exaltation possible nor of course any merit to make it necessary, although, on the other hand, it certainly put no hindrance in His way that could make it impossible.   It is to this *freedom* of grace that the miracle of the resurrection points, and not otherwise than by this sign do we have this " matter," do we have this gracious freedom of God and therefore the mystery of Easter before our eyes.   And this mystery is *grace*.   For most certainly that free undeserved act of God's sovereignty—possible only with God, but with God not impossible—in His Son as the first-born among many brethren affects us.   Most certainly all that is true in its concealment in Christ is true for us, as our real life. And again it is to this *grace* of the free God that the miracle of the resurrection points, as also those forty days that the apostles lived with their Lord in this world of ours and yet in the new time of God.   To deny this sign would mean to deny also the thing signified.   We have every reason for looking up to this sign with adoring gratitude.

XI

ASCENDIT AD COELOS, SEDET AD DEXTERAM DEI PATRIS OMNIPOTENTIS

IT may well be asked why the early Church came to
admit the Ascension amongst the main articles of
the Christian faith. In the New Testament it is
mentioned much less frequently and emphatically and
so had a much less conspicuous place than the death
and resurrection of Christ. It could even be omitted
from the testimony to the forty days as is shown by the
conclusion of the Gospels of Matthew and John, and also
by the genuine conclusion of the Gospel of Mark. Where
it is mentioned, it appears as a natural but not emphasised transition from the resurrection of Christ to
His " session at the Right Hand of God," which the
symbol also stresses later. We shall do well, also, to
view it first in this context, in order then, perhaps, to
understand how just *in* this context, just as such a
transition, it does in fact belong to the main articles of
the Christian faith.

Christ's " session at the Right Hand of God " with
which we start is to be understood first of all simply
as an explanation of the clause about His resurrection
from the dead. There is a series of New Testament
passages (e.g. Rom. viii. 34 ; Eph. i. 20 ; 1 Pet. iii. 22)
in which it stands alongside of the Easter witness quite
clearly with this purpose in view. And there are other

passages, especially in the Epistle to the Hebrews (i. 3 ; viii. 1 ; x. 12 ; xii. 2), where after the testimony to the suffering and death of Jesus, the Easter testimony itself, and as such, is comprehended and expressed in the clause dealing with His exaltation to the right hand of God. What the ten thousand times ten thousand angels (Rev. v. 12) say " with a loud voice " has obviously its place here : " Worthy is the Lamb that was slain to receive power, and riches, and wisdom, and strength, and honour, and glory, and blessing."

Let us attempt to analyse what the " session at the Right Hand of God " expresses. It states pictorially the truth, which from its very nature cannot be represented, that the might and sovereignty of God is in act and fact identical with the might and sovereignty of Him Who as true God became true man and Who as such died upon the Cross : Jesus Christ. It is therefore a figure of speech. In contradistinction to the *Conf. Helv. post.* Calvin hit the mark when in the " session at the Right Hand of God " he did not find anything said about Jesus Christ's being in a definite *place*, but about His having a definite *function*, namely, that of the exercise of divine power, comparable with that of a plenipotentiary who, standing or sitting at the right hand of his king, directs the government in his name. The fact that the symbol, in common with the majority of New Testament passages, speaks in that place of a " *session* " of Jesus Christ has nothing to do with the idea of blissful rest or the like. Rather it describes the continuance, the permanence of this function. What the figure states, that the Kingdom of God is in act and fact Kingdom of Christ, is not merely something that *has been*, but something that is and *continues*. By the additional words carried over from the first article, . . . of God " the Father Almighty," the symbol conclusively underlines the confession that the majesty, might and power that it ascribes to Christ have not merely a quasi-divine character, a character that is therefore in reality conditioned and circumscribed, but that on the contrary they are the genuine, eternal and sole majesty, might and power of God. The sovereignty of Jesus Christ is exercised in the full power of the Creator God. " *All* power is given unto Me in heaven and in earth " (Matt. xxviii. 18). That does not mean—the figure must not be pressed to the point of being misunderstood—that the eternal Father has now renounced this power and its exercise. We must not forget that it was not only with His resurrection or ascension that it was made over to Jesus Christ as the eternal Son of God. In so far as Jesus Christ is God Himself, neither in His Incarnation as such nor in His passion and death did He cease even for a moment to sit " at the Right Hand of God the Father ". And as certainly as His heavenly Father also is on less than God Himself, in no sense can there be any word of even a withdrawal on His part from the exercise of divine might. What the Creed says is said of Jesus Christ as the Son of God become *flesh*, become *man*. In the explanation that is here given of the clause about Christ's resurrection from the dead, what is new is that He as such, that is, in our nature and of our race, He as the bearer of our sin and guilt, as the companion of our fate, is at God's right hand, and therefore in possession and exercise of the one undivided power of God. But, even in this concrete relationship to the Son of God become man, this is really something new only in so far as it expresses the *revelation* of what began to be true

107

with the Incarnation and has never since ceased to be
true. Indeed it must be said, even of the Son of God
become man, that even as such, living, suffering and
dying, He had not *to be* raised to the right hand of the
Father, but already *was* the one Raised to the Father's
right hand ; only that He was not manifest as being
just that, but (with the exception of those " signs " of
His glory) was hidden, concealed, shut off from the eyes
of the world, nay, even from the eyes of His chosen and
called disciples. What happens in the " raising " of
Christ in His resurrection from the dead is that He is
now manifest in His supreme sovereignty. With the
revelation of the secret divine act of power that *took
place* on Good Friday, there *follows* on the heels of Good
Friday as a second, *new* day, Easter Day. But as we
have heard, Good Friday's divine act of power con-
sisted in this : that the Son of God turned, in Himself
as a true man, the wrath and curse of God that lay
upon man into blessing, the punishment into freedom,
the ordeal into victory. This divine act of power is
revealed by the risen Christ. It is therefore also the
content of the message of His witnesses, the " witnesses
of His resurrection " : " God was in Christ reconciling
the world unto Himself " (2 Cor. v. 14). And it is
just the power that makes this act possible and actual
that is meant in the *sedet ad dexteram Dei.* It is the
omnipotence of God the Father and the Son which
also belongs to the Son become man, hidden at first
and then manifest. In what God *does* there is made
manifest to us what God *wills* and thereby what God
can, the totality of His power. Even what God as
Creator can do, wills to do, and does is to be learned
here and only here. Now in retrospect we appreciate

why already in our explanation of the first article we had to understand the omnipotence of God as His power over life and death. Only that this has now for us a fuller content : it is God's power to kill and make alive, to exercise judgment and grace, to make the human cosmos grow old, that is, pass away and when it has passed away, to awaken it to new life. It is this power that operates in the work of salvation that is the power over life and death, which we adore and praise as God's omnipotence, as God's creative power. And this power of salvation is just that divine power of Jesus Christ exercised on Good Friday, and revealed on Easter Day or in the forty days.

Since there were men who in these forty days heard, saw, looked upon, handled the Risen One (1 John i. 1), this divine power of Jesus Christ *became history*, in order to *make* history, or better : in these men it *became Church*, assembly of believers, in order to *found* the Church through these men, e.g. through that Peter to whom the Father in heaven revealed Jesus Christ as Son of the living God (Matt. xvi. 18). There exists, therefore, an immediate and indissoluble connection between the *sessio ad dexteram* and—the Church, the body of which He is the Head (Col. i. 18). But the Church is the assembly of *those* men who have been called to faith by Christ's resurrection or by the witness borne to it, that is, however, called to the *acknowledgment* that the Gospel is just this : δύναμις θεοῦ εἰς σωτηρίαν (Rom. i. 16), which again means, called to *submission* to this " power of God unto salvation ". The assembly of these men is therefore separated and distinguished from the rest of humanity by Christ's crucifixion being known in it as the act of the *Son of God*, and this divine act as the act of the *reconciliation* of the world with God, and this act of reconciliation as an *act of power* performed once and for all. The last-mentioned is decisive at this point : the reconciliation becomes manifest among men as power, which implies that it dominates them, that it is meant for them, that it is the light, the truth of their existence, or in other words, that they exist only on the assumption, which they themselves have recognised, affirmed and accepted, that it is *for them* and to that extent actually *in them* that there took place in Christ the change from curse to blessing, from punishment to freedom, from ordeal to victory. Reconciliation as power over men in its publication (and so the Resurrection or the Resurrection message) is the event that founds the Church, and not only founds but also upholds it, and not only upholds but also renews it. As the Risen One, Christ is Lord of His Church, calls and carries it, leads and rules it, once and for all, yet also daily anew. The three offices of Christ differentiated by the older Dogmatics run into each other at this place so as to be almost indistinguishable. The *Prophet* (for what is the resurrection but the decisive act of Jesus Christ's prophecy ?) announces the *Priest* (Who appears for man before God, for God before man) in order to proclaim Him as such, *King*. Where that is said, heard and believed, there is the Church. The Church is the special and peculiar sphere of this third office, the **munus regium Christi**. It is for the sake of the Church, i.e. of His sovereignty over it and in it, because of the power and care that He desires to exercise in this assembly, that Christ sits at the right hand of the Father. His power, acknowledged, and ever and again to be acknowledged, in the preaching and faith of the Church, His power to kill and to make alive, to exercise grace and judgment, to make the old things pass away and a new creature appear (2 Cor. v. 17)—that power is the power of His death exhibited in His resurrection. It is therefore to that end, in this function which His Church proclaims and in which it believes, that he sits at the right hand of God the Father. " What benefit do we receive from this glory of our Head, Christ ? First, that by His Holy Spirit He sheds forth heavenly gifts in us, His members. Then, that by His power He defends and preserves us against all enemies " (Heidelberg Catechism, Q. 51). We shall have occasion to remind ourselves of this at a decisive point in the third article of the Creed.

Let us mark this also. In showing the direct relationship of the sovereignty of Christ to the reconciliation accomplished in Him, on the one hand, and to the Church that is grounded in Him, on the other, it must not be overlooked or denied that besides a realm of grace there is also a realm of creation. This realm is abandoned neither to itself nor to other gods nor to an unknown God. On the contrary here no less than there all divine power is possessed and exercised by Jesus Christ as the eternal Son of God. Our Reconciler and the Lord of the Church is He Who is the Creator of the world, Who from the beginning of the world right on to its end is also its absolute Lord. " *All* things were made by Him " (John i. 3)—not primarily and not only the Church. Poor Church that would fail to keep this in mind in naming Him her Lord ! And poor world that would fail to have its very own Lord proclaimed to it by the Church ! Moreover, it must not be overlooked and denied that the realm of grace has its natural frontier in a forward direction also, but that this again cannot signify any limitation of the sovereignty of Christ. Reconciliation, and with it the Church, is not the ultimate but the penultimate divine order. The ultimate order, the order of the realm of *glory* in which, on the basis of the atonement man's redemption is reached, is again not identical with any Church reality, but the goal of all Church reality, because the goal of Christ as Reconciler and as Lord of the Church (1 Cor. xv. 25 f.). Once again, poor Church that failed to know its Lord as the coming Lord of glory ! And poor world, if the Church, which has so much fighting to do *in* it and often enough *against* it, were not as place of conflict to be also, with its Lord in view, a place of hope ! But we must not allow this double reservation to confuse us. As long as time lasts, we stand in the realm of *grace* and therefore do not know the *munus regium Christi* otherwise than in the *munus propheticum* that proclaims to us His *munus sacerdotale*. We do not have God the Creator and God the finisher of all things otherwise than as God our reconciler. As pardoned sinners we have Him. His realm amongst us is the spiritual realm of His Word that kills and makes alive. The man who wants to have Him here and now and otherwise is either a sophist or a fanatic. Neither of these shall we be. But to have the Lord of nature and history and the Lord of glory we shall hold by the Lord of the *Church*. As that He is Alpha and Omega. As that He holds in His hands as Mediator both the beginning and the end.

This puts us into the position from which we should be able to give an account of the meaning of the Ascension. So much is certain, that it, too, is to be estimated first of all as the " sign and wonder " that accompanies the secret of the Christian faith in the act of its revelation. Ascension as visible exaltation—i.e. exaltation that is perceptible as vertical elevation in space—of Jesus Christ before the bodily eyes of His disciples is obviously not the way to that session at the right hand of God. For the right hand of God is no place, least of all a place to be reached by some sort of natural or supernatural way through atmospheric astronomic space. As sign and wonder this exaltation is a *pointer* to the revelation, that occurred in His resurrection, of Jesus Christ as the bearer of all power in heaven and earth. From this aspect the Ascension is nothing else than the concluding form, and as such the most concrete, of those appearances of the Risen One in the forty days, by means of which the previously hidden Son of God discloses Himself, by means of which He creates the faith of His disciples and so creates the Church. From this point of view the significance of the Ascension is identical with the significance both of the resurrection and the *Sessio ad dexteram.* And so, also, the answers to Questions 45, 49 and 51 in the Heidelberg Catechism manifestly have in reality one and the same content.

But the Ascension can and must be regarded from still another point of view, and thereby what is peculiar to it becomes visible. It was Calvin who laid special stress on this other point of view. For he saw in the Ascension not only the crowning conclusion, but above all the *end* of these appearances of the Risen One. Therefore, in strange contrast to the promise, " Lo, I am with you alway, even unto the end of the world " (Matt. xxviii. 20), he saw the fulfilment of the word, " But Me ye have not always " (Matt. xxvi. 11). God's revelation having taken place once and for all in Christ, the Ascension makes a separation, a distance between Him and His disciples, between Him and the world generally. Ended is the time of His direct, His " worldly " presence in the world, to which the forty days unmistakably belonged. There dawns—one could also say, there returns, the time of the *Church*. In that time, too, we can speak of His presence in the world, the world which has already been overcome by the mighty saving act of His cross and in which He has once and for all shown Himself as conqueror. But it is His presence in a world, with which God still has patience, to which He therefore allows time, a temporal future, room for *knowledge* of His having overcome it, room for *faith* in the mighty saving act of the Cross revealed in the resurrection. This time is therefore and to that extent a time of His very real but also very indirect presence. As Calvin and the Heidelberg Catechism, Questions 47 and 48, and all Reformed Theology have rightly taught, it is the time in which Jesus Christ is present as God *and* man, to the world *and* to the Church, only through the Holy Ghost in the witnesses to and in the attestation of His revelation, in which His Kingdom therefore is a divinely real, but, as already stated, a *spiritual* Kingdom. It is the time in which revealed reconciliation or reconciling revelation is to be acknowledged and adored and believed in as God's free grace. It is no longer and not yet the time of the " beholding of His glory " (John i. 14 ; cf. 2 Cor. v. 7). It is the time *between* the times, namely, between the time of revelation and the time, announced in and with revelation, of seeing face to face (1 Cor. xiii. 12) which will also be the end of time. The time of revelation is the anticipation of the end of all times (John v. 25 ; Heb. i. 2 ; 1 Pet. i. 20). To that extent the Kingdom of God " is close at hand " (Mark i. 15). And whereas revelation is proclaimed and believed, there, in the light of this anticipation of its end, time becomes finite ; becomes, in short, a time that is left to us merely by God's patience, and is designed and fitted precisely to afford opportunity for faith ; becomes in short, directed to the end (the Eschaton) or rather to Him Who is the end (the Eschatos) and Who stands before the door and knocks (1 Pet. iv. 2 ; 1 John ii. 18). This time is the time of the Church. The Church is the *earthly* body of its *heavenly* head. With this relative difference and opposition it is one with Him. It is one with Him through revelation and in faith. Through His *Holy Spirit* it participates in the act of power and salvation that He performed, and therefore participates in the Kingdom that is close at hand, by way of *obedience* and *hope*, in submission to His mediatorial office in confidence in His *substitution* and *advocacy* with the Father, in dependence upon the *gifts* of His mercy. It is just this mediateness that is the boundary of the Church and of the whole time of the Church. The Church is an assembly of sinful and mortal *men* who as such have by grace dealings with *God the Lord*, and therefore must watch and pray, wait and make haste, suffer and fight. Its time is not simply the continuation of the time of revelation. If it were that, it would already be the final age (*Endzeit*), and we should be living already in eternal glory, by sight and not by faith. It was thus that the first witnesses in the forty days lived. No longer do we live thus, or not yet. The time of the Church is the *interim period* which has its origin in the revelation period, which gives us room for repentance and which is in keeping with the proximity of the Kingdom of God. That is the boundary of this period, the boundary which is also the door upon which Jesus Christ (Who *has* come and Who likewise *will* come again in direct worldly presence) knocks, and so knocking is with us alway even unto the end of the world. The *beginning* of this time with all those things that condition and define it concretely, with its boundary and with its outlook, is the *Ascension*. It has significance from this point of view alongside of the Resurrection. From this point of view it may perhaps be characterised together with the Virgin Birth and with the *sepultus* as the *critical* point in the Creed. It reminds the Church founded by the resurrection that as such it stands under the Cross, which means, in the concealment of God which He Himself alone breaks through when it pleases Him. It reminds it that the relationship of head and body is not reversible, that the healing omnipotence is the power of the *Lord :* it is *over* us and *for us* but without ever becoming *our* power. It reminds it of the patience of God, but at the same time of His claim, under which it exists as Church. It places it under the law of humility. It is most certainly no denial, interruption or retraction of the Easter message of peace between God and Man. But *for the sake of this peace* it admonishes and warns : " Seek the things that are above " (Col. iii. 1). It is to that extent the exact counterpart of the miracle of the Virgin Birth which says the same thing from the other side : that it is the " dayspring from on high " which has visited us in Jesus Christ (Luke i. 78).

XII

INDE VENTURUS EST IUDICARE
VIVOS ET MORTUOS

THESE words that conclude the second article give
us confirmation of the fact that in our explanation of the Ascension from the second point of
view we took what was essentially a right line. Following the long row of *Perfects, conceptus, natus, passus,
crucifixus, mortuus, sepultus est, resurrexit, ascendit,* and
the *Present* that stands over against that row, *sedet ad
dexteram Dei,* there comes now a *Future, venturus est.*
That means : the Church, whose faith is confessed in
the Creed, looks backwards and also forwards. It has
a past and a future. It remembers and it waits. It
exists therefore in a *temporal* present. In this present
it is constituted Church by that *sedet ad dexteram Dei,*

From that *sedet ad dexteram Dei,* from the Lordship
of Jesus Christ manifest in the present and known and
affirmed in faith, it looks *back.* Viewed from this point,
the time of revelation described in these statements in
the Perfect tense is of course not *past.* Rather as time
of revelation it is present to the Church in and with the
Lordship of Christ that governs the Church. And each
remembrance of it as such signifies recognition and
affirmation of its being thus present. So far as the
Church lives by revelation and in faith, it lives con-
temporaneously with the divine act depicted in these
Perfects. Therefore looking back to revelation time we

see that the time of the unreconciled man *has* passed
with this divine act and *appears* as past. This time of
the unreconciled man is that time of Pontius Pilate of
which we have spoken, i.e. our world time in which
Jesus Christ had to suffer and did suffer, under which,
it goes without saying, we have to understand just as
much the time after Christ as that before Christ, so far
as it is world time. This world time was concluded by
Jesus Christ in His death by the dawn of *His* time, God's
time as the time of man reconciled by Him to God. The
contemporaneousness in which the Church lives with the
mighty saving act accomplished in Christ, has its reverse
side ; its noncontemporaneousness with the man of
disobedience and disorder overcome in Christ. Looked
at from that present, he still exists only as the in principle
" old " man (Rom. vi. 6). And to the degree that he
does go on existing as that " old " man, and therefore
" still " has time, to the degree that his time, concluded
in the death of Christ, is itself still time, having a present
and therefore also a future—to that degree will the
Christian (so far as he is a contemporary of Christ !)
and the Church (so far as it lives by revelation and in
faith !) always be able to exist only *un*seasonably, i.e.
not in conformity with this time that in both its dimen-
sions has passed away in Christ.

But from that Present, *sedet ad dexteram Dei*, the Church
now looks *forwards* also. But what it looks forward to
cannot be any sort of neutral future, nor yet the content
of a present of world time that has not yet come to pass
and that is either near at hand or still far off. In the
Cross of Christ that time, with all its past, present and
future possibilities, is in its totality concluded and become
past. In it, that is, in the development of events that we

call world history, the Church has nothing to expect except the " signs of the time," i.e. the indications of its being past and therefore the indications of the real *future*, distinguished from a mere futurity. What this real future is and what therefore the object of the actual and earnest expectation of the Church is follows immediately and cogently from its present as that is constituted by the Lordship of Christ. This present, as we saw, means *contemporaneousness*, the having of Jesus Christ as a contemporary. In this present the divine power is *operative*. In this present, therefore, the Church remembers revelation time. But it is not possible merely to remember revelation time. When it is really remembered, then it is also *expected*. And the divine power of Christ's resurrection cannot be merely operative. Where it is operative, it also becomes at once promise and hope. And contemporaneousness with Jesus Christ cannot merely consist in His not being past for us, but rather in His being present. If He is that, then He is also future for us. If He has come, then He will come also, *venturus est*. Why should all that be ? We can only answer : because He is Jesus Christ, the true God Who assumed true humanity, and Who in His humiliation and exaltation was victorious in this humanity, i.e. changed sin into righteousness, and death into life. If in virtue of His revelation we are the men adopted by Him as God, i.e. if in faith we know and confess ourselves as members of the humanity assumed by Him, if we are in the Church, i.e. amongst the number of those chosen, called and gathered by Him, then *He* is the content of our time and that not only of our present but also of our *future*. He cannot be content of our present without thereby becoming content of our future also. Only if we fell away from the state in which we were adopted by

119

Him, that is fell away from the belief that as true God He adopted true humanity and reconciled it with God, only if we denied the mystery of Christmas and of Good Friday, could we be free to look for another (Matt. xi. 3), free for a future that would not be His future. On the strength of His revelation, hanging upon Him in faith, we know the time as in Him " fulfilled " time (Mk. i. 15 ; Gal. iv. 4). What sort of a future would that be, which could be our future *instead* of Him or *alongside* of Him ? Our sole future is that *He* will come, just as our sole present is that He has come. By virtue of His kingly office, as that became visible in His resurrection, the Church is in the position of having no other future than that which it acknowledges in the prayer : Amen ; come, Lord Jesus ! By virtue of His kingly office it *has* this future. *Venturus est* therefore means : Christ is our *hope*, and—*Christ* is our hope.

Now the symbol attaches this clause to what precedes : *Inde venturus*. The statement of the Whence of the Lord's coming obviously refers first of all to the "right hand of God " which was previously characterised as the position to which Jesus Christ was raised in His resurrection and Ascension. We saw that this did not mean a place but a function, and so in confirmation of what has just been set forth we can rewrite the clause in this way : by virtue of His possession and exercise of His divine *omnipotence*, as that was made manifest in His resurrection, Jesus Christ is not only He Who is and was, but as such, He also Who is to come (Rev. i. 4). He is coming because the time which by the patience of God is allowed as room for repentance to the old man and so also to the Church is in its nature a time that is passed away and indeed a time relegated by His resurrection to the past and therefore a time to which *He* Himself forms the frontier. So far as it is still our time, we must say of it that it is in *His* hands, that it is held by *Him* right from the end as from the beginning, that therefore, beyond all its future contents, it has its future in *Him*. The *inde venturus* can then be rendered by the Old Testament word : the right hand of the Lord *achieves* the victory ! (Ps. cxviii. 15).

But the *inde* certainly points back at the same time to the " heaven " to which, according to the preceding clause of the Creed, Jesus Christ ascended, to the divine height, to the " above " within which in the intermediate period of patience, in the time of the Church, He is hidden from the bodily as from the incorporeal eyes of man, even of those who believe in Him. We shall hardly err if we understand this interim period as a repetition of the humiliation of the Lord Himself. The Church—and *its* time is indeed this interim period—will, with its preaching, its sacrament, its faith, always be the Church under the *Cross*. So *inde venturus* means also, that Jesus Christ comes from just there, i.e. He returns from the conceal-ment into which He there entered. The Second Coming of Christ is the restoration, but at the same time the universal and final revelation, of the direct presence of Jesus Christ as " God-man," as that was the content of the forty days after Easter. " He comes again in the clouds of heaven with power and great glory " as we read, Matt. xxiv. 30 ; and a little before : "As the lightning cometh out of the east and shineth even unto the west, so shall be the presence of the Son of Man " (Matt. xxiv. 27). The interim period in which the old man as such *still* continued to exist, having his own future, the time of the Church, of preaching and of sacrament and of faith is then not only in itself concluded—it is that now—but has also run out, become

futureless. Then, as we read in Rev. xi. 15, " the kingdoms of this *world* are become the kingdoms of our Lord
and of His Christ " immediately, undialectically, incon-
trovertibly, irresistibly. They become that as immediately
as He in His Incarnation made human nature and human
fate His own, in order by His death to make them a new
creature. Then He will be not only the Reconciler, then
He will be the Redeemer, the Saviour of the world (Tit.
ii. 13). On a second and final comprehensive Easter Day
the exaltation of the Lord will be repeated. The interim
period is running towards that Easter as the Day of the
Lord. The Church with all creatures in their sighing is,
in this interim period, waiting and watching joyfully for
that day.

This, I think clears the way for the understanding of a
further point. That is, that the significance of the Second
Coming of Christ is, in harmony with the New Testament,
indicated by the words *iudicare vivos et mortuos*. Some
might have scruples at this point. We have already
called Christ not only our future but with great assurance also our *hope*. In doing so have we not said something
that we can say only with the greatest qualification, something indeed that we cannot perhaps say at all ? When
He comes again as Judge, could He not, yes must He not
of necessity be our *fear* rather than our hope ? We think
of the passage from the familiar mediæval hymn : *cum
vix iustus sit securus, quid sum miser tunc dicturus ?* We
think of Michelangelo's representation of Christ as Judge
of the World in His Second Advent and of so many others
that notoriously rouse terror. In contrast to that how
strikingly do the 52nd Question and Answer of the Heidelberg Catchism sound ! " What *comfort* is it to thee that
Christ shall come again to judge the quick and the dead ?

That in all my sorrows and persecutions, with uplifted head, I look for the self-same One Who has before offered Himself for me to the judgment of God, and removed from me all curse, to come again as Judge from heaven : Who shall cast all His and my enemies into everlasting condemnation, but shall take me and all His chosen ones to Himself, into eternal joy and glory." Let it be granted that that could be said in a way that comes dangerously near to arrogant self-assurance. Yet as a matter of fact it is said here absolutely rightly. It cannot be made clear enough that the Judge Whom we go to meet (or rather Who comes to meet us as our future !) is not any judge, not even anyone equipped with divine power of judgment and punishment. Regard is not paid to the seriousness of the judgment of Jesus Christ if it is not expected strictly as *His* judgment, but just on that account " with uplifted head " and " comforted " by the prospect of this future. The returning Christ is not feared as He certainly wants to be feared, if it is not first and foremost and unconditionally recognised : He is our hope. We can easily accept the *dies irae, dies illa* and Michelangelo's World-judgment as very apt descriptions of faith fighting with the (" still " existing) " old " man, of the strife between spirit and flesh in the interim period. But *these* are the melodies and the pictures that are simply *not* appropriate to Christ's Second Advent which puts an end to this interim period and brings the dawn of the kingdom of glory. For Jesus Christ really comes from heaven as He Who sits at the right hand of God, therefore as the Risen One, therefore as the Revealer of the reconciliation accomplished in Him, therefore as He Who has accomplished this reconciliation, and therefore in fact as the Judge Who anticipated the judgment for us and through Whose punishment we are righteous. Dare we forget that and cancel it out in favour of an abstract divine, or rather all-too-human, figure of a judge ? It is just from this figure of a judge, and that means, from an arbitrary law placed before the Gospel and ranged above it, that man has always been fleeing with the terror that such a situation creates. But here is the Judge from Whom no one can flee : the crucified Christ Who as the Risen One proclaims and exercises the absolute sovereignty of grace. Judgment means decision. And so the world judgment also is *decision*, the decision, which is made upon all in Church and world, upon the living and upon the dead, i.e. directly upon all men of all times, which excludes, annuls, annihilates every reserve and contradiction, the ultimate decision of *Good Friday* that comes down from *heaven*, the decision that man is justified and saved by the Son of God and without Him is condemned and lost. How should the man who believes in Him and therefore in God's unmerited grace, and who (observe !) does the good works that *this* faith implies—how should such a man not really look to *this* Judge " with uplifted head " even if all the other judges in heaven and earth should condemn him with thousand-fold justice ? Just that man and only that man has knowledge of the depth of human sin and guilt, of God's burning wrath, of the severity of His punishment, who realises that it has all been borne and borne away by Christ. From what other source should a knowledge of that be got ? All knowledge of sin that did not come from faith in God's grace, that was not knowledge in Christ, was still imbued with secret self-righteousness. *That* Judge is really feared of Whom it is known that His grace is our *single* hope, but really our *hope*. This Judge is Christ in His Second Advent. He, in Whom the compassion of

God has conquered in human nature, *He* divides in that He decides, He sets the sheep on the right hand, the goats on the left, He rewards the doers of good works and punishes the doers of evil works, He leads into eternal joy and hurls into eternal torment. Truly, having to face this decision and division is not a jesting matter. But the seriousness of this judgment is the *divine* and not any merely human seriousness, even the highest religious and moral or the profoundest theological seriousness. Here the first become the last and the last the first and the measure used for measuring will be the actual value of free grace in our life and therefore no human measure. Observe, even the best theological camouflage and entrenchments will not help us. Not all the orthodox, not all the pietists, not even all the followers of Kohlbrügge will enter heaven! The eyes of the Son of God will always see a good deal more sharply than any human eyes. Probably even alleged publicans who could never get their fill of praising " grace, the whole of grace and nothing but grace," are here unmasked as Pharisees, and all sorts of apparent Pharisees with a publican-heart that only God knew will go down to their house justified. Work-righteousness, which is after all to be recognised as the one, real, unpardonable sin, the sin against the Holy Ghost, is always a little more obscure in actual fact than one might well suppose it to be. Before the judgment-seat of Christ it will not remain hidden. Here each will be repaid according to his works, according to the faith or the unbelief that he actually lives out. The *faith* or *unbelief* in God's compassion, but that, not according to any ever so fine display of the one or the other, but according to what is *actually* lived out !

What Christ's Second Advent and His judgment of the

quick and the dead signify and will import to us is—this
decision over us, this division between us, the eternal, the
radical and final decision and division. How could that
day and that judgment be anything but dreadful ? Yet
that cannot be Christian teaching, that we must be afraid,
or half afraid and half hopeful. Here we can only hope
and indeed hope without reserve. For the day and the
judgment that we go to meet are the day of Jesus Christ
and the judgment of Jesus Christ. Only *hope* and that the
hope which is centred solely and entirely in Him, will save
us on that day and in that judgment ! But *fear* of Him—
yes, what other kind of fear could this be than the fear
that one may be found, on that day and in that judgment,
to be without the hope that is placed solely and entirely
in Him ?

XIII

CREDO IN SPIRITUM SANCTUM

A GLANCE over the content of this third article that now lies before us compels us first of all to make the following remarks :—

1. It is *man* who now moves into the visual field of the Creed. Already in discussing the first and second articles we have had most emphatically to speak of man, of his sin and reconciliation, and of the claim and the promise under which he is placed, and that for the reason that the first and second articles are followed, in a position of equal importance and emphasis, by this third article and that it is impossible for us rightly to understand and elucidate the first and the second except in the closest connection with this third. There is, so we are told here, a Church, that is, a holy assembly, for holy fellowship. There is a forgiveness of sins. There is a resurrection of the flesh. There is an eternal life. Not only for God, and also not only for the Mediator Jesus Christ, but for *us*, for *man*, is what is meant. If, in spite of all that was said in this direction in our exposition of the first and second articles, anyone went to sleep under the impression that we were dealing there with matters all too high, all too far off and unpractical, he is now requested to waken up, for the cry now is, *Tua res agitur*, the whole time is given to discussion of what is lowest, nearest, most actual, namely ourselves.

2. Of course it would have been much better not to

go to sleep at all. It would have been better to have the content of the first and second articles clearly in our minds if we are now to take in the third article. In that article we are not (as might perhaps be expected) at long last going to see, as over against the confession of God the Creator and His work of reconciliation, a doctrine of man, an anthropology. Nor, we must hasten to add, either a general philosophical or even a special Christian anthropology. The word *credo* is repeated just here by way of warning. I do not think that that is done merely for stylistic reasons. I think we are to be reminded that here again and just here we are concerned not with a human view, but with God's revelation, not with an " article of sight " but with an " article of faith." Man's entering the visual field does not mean that *he* now becomes the theme, that what comes to utterance now are *his* questions and problems, that we can now impatiently listen to hear whether in those human concerns which, for this reason and that, are important to *us*, we are at last to get our rights and come out solvent. Anyone listening only on this condition would soon go to sleep again and that for good. For the way in which, in the third article, we speak about man is this. We speak of the *Holy Spirit*, we speak of the Church, of forgiveness of sins, of the resurrection of the flesh and of eternal life, but just because and in so far as man gets a share in all that through the Holy Spirit. Therefore what is spoken of is the concern of *God* for man, not the reverse. Let us take note of what thereby becomes of our concerns! The Creed is, and even at this place remains, *theological*. An anthropology, that is, a system of propositions with man for its subject is not to be abstracted from what is here said about man. Nor, accordingly, any ethic—unless a theological ethic which would have the task not of *answering* all sorts of " moral " questions but rather first and foremost of *raising* and *urging* just those questions which are put to man by the divine concern.

3. The third article as doctrine of the Holy Spirit and of what man obtains through Him, obviously stands over against the *second* article as the doctrine of *Christ* and His work in a special direct relationship. There is such a thing as a Church, because Jesus Christ is our Lord, sitting at the right hand of God—forgiveness of sins, because Jesus Christ was crucified and died—resurrection of the flesh, because Jesus Christ rose from the dead— eternal life, because He comes again to judge the quick and the dead. Here nothing counts by itself, everything only in this relationship. We can say in advance that even the Holy Spirit Himself is in exactly the same position. He is the *Holy* Spirit because He is the Spirit of Jesus Christ. But clearly the reverse of this is also true. It is possible to speak rightly of Christ only if and while we are also speaking of the Holy Spirit and His work, and therefore of man, which means of Church, forgiveness of sins, resurrection of the dead and eternal life. From the fact of this connection we gather that what the Creed in conjunction with Holy Scripture wants to certify as God's revelation, does not on the one side confine itself to what happened once and for all, the fact of Christ in itself, but includes in this something that happens to many men at many times—and, on the other side, will not suffer itself to be limited by the human experiences of the various other times in which it is received and accepted as revelation. Nay, but the one actual, divine revelation has, as it were, an objective

and a subjective side. It would not be the actual divine revelation if it were merely, so to speak, an objective divine performance, out of which men could then make what is possible and permissible according to some other prescription. But no less and nothing else than actual divine revelation is also the subjective side, i.e. the participation men get and take in it. With the reserve, which the philosophical overloading of these conceptions makes necessary, we can say : the doctrine of *Christ* points to the *objective*, the doctrine of the *Holy Spirit* to the *subjective* side of this reality. To which we add again that, while we have to distinguish the two, we have not for a moment or in any respect to separate them.

The clear Biblical fundamental doctrine of the work of the Holy Spirit which the symbol has in view with its *credo in Spiritum sanctum* is that the revelation of the Father in the Son is the revelation through the Holy Spirit. We say exactly the same thing when we say that the reconciliation of the world to God in Christ is the reconciliation through the Holy Spirit. By Holy Spirit is to be understood : God Who comes to man and indeed comes to him in such a way that He is *known* to him, that man lets himself be reconciled, in other words, that he *believes* in God's Word and Son Jesus Christ. As the $\pi\nu\epsilon\hat{\upsilon}\mu\alpha$, i.e. as the wind, goes from here to there, as the breath of our mouth goes from one to the other, so God as Holy Spirit goes out from Himself to man, yes, right into man, in order to make him open, free, ready for, capable to receive, Himself, that is, His Son, His Word. Man *needs* to be made open and free for God's revelation and reconciliation. He is not already that in himself. The Holy Ghost by effecting revelation

130

and reconciliation makes it impossible for us to cherish the thought that we are open for God, that we could prepare and get ourselves ready for this event. " I believe that I cannot by my own reason and strength believe in Jesus Christ my Lord or come to Him " (Luther). Accordingly, he who believes, knows that even this—the fact that he *believes*, is God's work and gift ; knows that He cannot see the ground in himself of his faith, cannot understand it as his doing, but again can only—believe. In believing, a man lets himself be told that he not only *commits* sin but *is* a sinner, that is, a rebel against grace and as such incapable of the decision of faith. If it is nevertheless true that he believes, then that means that a miracle has taken place in him. That will be accomplished in the shape of all sorts of definite events and experiences ; certainly he will acquire in the process all sorts of definite insights, will make all sorts of definite resolutions and no doubt carry them out. But it will not be from his experiences, from his insights and resolutions, it will not be in any way out of himself that he will explain to himself the fact that he really believes, that he is therefore one to whom God is manifest, one who is reconciled with God. On the contrary, for the very fact that that journey from death to life which Christ accomplished affects him personally, he will give the glory to God Himself, as amazed and as thankful as he was before the cradle at Bethlehem and before the Cross at Golgotha. He who has learned to reverence free grace in the miracle of the Virgin Birth and in the miracle of the Ascension will reverence it all the more in the miracle that he—he who does *not* know himself as other than God's enemy, other than as contemner of grace, other than as one who openly or secretly trusts in works !—may in faith have peace with God, be called God's child, do the works of a pardoned man, go to meet his Judge with uplifted head. It will never occur to him to seek to understand himself as one who, acting in freedom and on the basis of that freedom, has achieved all that. He will understand and glory in God's freedom, the freedom of *grace*, in which he has had all that bestowed upon him. " No man can say that Jesus is Lord but by the Holy Spirit " (1 Cor. xii. 3). " If any man have not the Spirit of Christ, he is none of His " (Rom. viii. 9). He, " the Holy Spirit, has called me through the Gospel, enlightened me by His gifts, and sanctified and preserved me in the true faith, just as He calls, gathers, enlightens and sanctifies the whole Christian Church on earth and preserves it in union with Jesus Christ in the one true faith " (Luther).

Holy Scripture *distinguishes* the *Spirit* of God from the *Word* of God ; it distinguishes Him also from *Christ*. As in the one reality of revelation and reconciliation it is something *special* that God is not only veiled from us as the Father but is unveiled as the Son, so it is once more something *special* and new that on this road from concealment into the light of day God *imparts Himself to us, to us men*, takes us, so to speak, with Him on this way, which is at once the way from judgment to grace, from death to life, and so becomes manifest *to us*, so becomes *our* reconciler. Christ and His way from death to resurrection is the presupposition, is the objective in relation to which this subjective—certainly not as a matter of course, but as fulfilment of *special* promise after the significant pause between Ascension and Pentecost—becomes *event*, the " coming down " indeed the " falling down " of the Spirit upon those to whom the exalted Lord, sitting at the right hand of the Father, will " send " Him. It could well be asked whether the step which is once more made here in the revelation of the Spirit is not *still* greater, more astonishing, stranger than the step from Good Friday to Easter, from the revelation of the Father to the revelation of the Son. It is at least *equally* great. And so we understand the necessity for solemnly introducing the Holy Spirit in the symbol with *credo*, for expressly marking Him out also as object of faith. In believing that Christ is God's Son we must again and specially believe, must start out by believing, in the work of God that is visible in the *fact that* we believe !

We have just spoken of the " revelation of the Spirit ". But as the revelation of the Son in His resurrection has no other content than the hidden will of the Father which already triumphed in Christ's Cross and death, so also the revelation of the Spirit can add nothing to the revelation in Jesus Christ. " He shall glorify Me : for He shall receive of *Mine* and shall show it unto you " (John xvi. 14). That—and it is truly great, real and marvellous enough when one reflects Who God in Jesus Christ is, and who *we* are !—that and nothing else is the work of the Holy Spirit. He who thinks he is able to supplement and enrich the revelation that took place in Jesus Christ under the title " Spirit " with divers alleged divine truths drawn from nature and history, gained through reason or experience or even through immediate illumination, he will definitely lay himself open to the reproach that the Spirit to which he appeals is a different one from Him, Whom the Bible names *Holy* Spirit. This undertaking in all its forms has always ended with the attempt to proceed from supplementing and enriching to dispossessing and denying the revelation that took place in Jesus Christ. It is likely that the crucial question for the Evangelical Church and for theology to-day is just this : whether it will be granted to them to find, between the two great realms of fundamentally false doctrine about the Holy Spirit—namely, between Roman Catholicism and the New-Protestantism of the last 200 years that has its roots in mediæval and humanistic spiritualism—the way to knowledge and worship of the Holy Spirit as the Spirit of the *Word* of God. He, *Jesus,* " breathed on them, and saith unto them, Receive ye the Holy Spirit ! " (John xx. 22). We have sufficient in this Spirit. We have sufficient in the Spirit Who is our guarantee and seal that *for Christ's sake* we can by grace be called and be what He is by nature : God's children. We have sufficient in the Spirit Who discloses *His* words and deeds, *His* cross and His resurrection to us, as the divine reality bearing upon us, embracing us, giving to us. We have sufficient in the Spirit Who in the Church's witness to *Him* gives to the ears of all sorts of people, with all sorts of languages, the witness of *divine* truth, that is, of divine simplicity and intelligibility. We have sufficient in this Spirit not because we did not also know various other spirits and in their way prize them, without at once having enough of them. But we do have, the Church of Jesus Christ does have, sufficient in Jesus Christ, in the Word of God that He Himself speaks and is, for the reason that to *its* questions He is the only One Who gives an answer. For God's revelation and reconciliation accomplished once and for all in Jesus Christ there is no substitute, however richly and beautifully the world, apart from it, may greet us. To it none of these other spirits, whatever name they bear, makes us accessible. They do not render us free from faith in grace. It is rather the evil secret of all other spirits, of all world-spirits, from the lowest to the highest, that at best they make us put our trust in works. On that account we cannot distinguish clearly enough the highest truth, power and wisdom of our spiritual world from *spiritual* truth, power and wisdom. On that account the Church confesses with absolute exclusiveness : *Credo in Spiritum sanctum.* On that account it means thereby the one only Spirit, the " Spirit of Jesus Christ," so called because it is from *Him* He comes and to *Him* He leads, because it is to *Him* He bears witness and of *Him* that He makes us witnesses. One need in fact be no narrow-minded fanatic, one need be no more than a man who faces facts in his thinking, to see that this is necessarily so.

And now in conclusion we can state it as self-evident, that when we speak of the Holy Ghost in the same way as prophets and apostles have done, we are speaking in the same emphatic and complete sense of *God Himself* as when we speak of Jesus Christ. The first centuries after the Apostolic age were longer in reaching clarity about this than in regard to the divinity of Christ. And it is sufficiently significant that the newer Protestantism has largely returned to the practice of speaking of the Holy Spirit as of a spiritual power belonging to history and bearing all the marks of creatureliness. But the Nicæno-Constantinopolitan Creed rightly calls Him the " Lord-Spirit " (πνεῦμα το ἅγιον, το κύριον) Who proceeds from the Father and the Son, Who with the Father and the Son together is worshipped and glorified. That is to say : the Holy Spirit of adoption, of revelation and of witness, the Holy Spirit Who makes us free for the Word of God, is *eternal* Spirit in the same way as the Father is *eternal* Father and as the Son is *eternal* Son. He is of one substance with Father and Son and therefore with Them the one true God, Creator, Reconciler and Redeemer. The decision that faith makes in regard to this clause of the Creed is made on entirely similar lines to that made in regard to the clause about the divinity of Jesus Christ. If the Holy Spirit is not Himself true God, in what sense then can we say : I *believe* in the Holy Spirit ? We should be wise to have nothing whatever to do with believing in a mere spiritual power. But if we realise the secret and the miracle of the fact that we *believe*, that it is really permissible and possible for us to believe in Jesus Christ and therefore in God, if it is plain to us that this permission and possibility are, according to John iii. 3, nothing less than a " new birth," then it cannot very long remain hidden from us that the power which achieves that in us cannot be anything less than *God's* power. God in Himself is the *love* which becomes visible in us in this mystery and miracle. In God Himself it is the love of the Father to the Son, of the Son to the Father. This eternal *love in God Himself* is the Holy Spirit, of Whose work this third article speaks.

XIV

SANCTAM ECCLESIAM CATHOLICAM, SANCTORUM COMMUNIONEM

WE shall be able to deal only very sketchily with the wealth of problems, perceptions and implications that crowd together in this part of the Confession.

Ecclesia is an *assembly* which has come into existence through a call. The Germanic equivalent *Kirche, kerk,* Church, is to my mind, not, as we are usually told, a truncated rendering of the Greek adjective, κυριακή (ἐκκλησία), but is to be referred to that stem to which, for example, the Latin vocables *circa, circum, circare, circulus,* etc., also belong. It describes therefore a *place* that is definite and bounded and to that extent made prominent. The New Testament itself really justifies our connecting these two explanations together. The Church is an assembly that has come into existence in a definite place. And on the other side, it is the place where an assembly has been held, and is to be held again and again. The supplementary clause *sanctorum communionem* can furnish us with a third formal mark : Church is a *community*, that is, it is an assembly or a place where all who belong to it have a common interest by which they are bound together into a unity.

Let us first of all attempt to define a little more precisely. In this part of the symbol the adjective *s a n c t u s* appears twice. It emphasises, first, the prominence, the special dignity and blessedness of this assembly, this place, this community, but also the special claim made upon it and the special commission entrusted to it. And, secondly, it emphasises, with perhaps intentional ambiguity, the peculiarity of the common concern, the *sancta* of this *communio*, and therewith the separation of those, the *sancti*, who belong to this *communio*. All of which means that as over against the Church—what it is concerned with, and those who belong to it—there stand other assemblies, places and communities from which it is *distinguished*. There is also a *communio* of marriage, of family, of people, of state, there are fellowships of race, culture and class, there are natural and contractual societies and unions, alliances and fellowships. Their legitimacy is not contested by the Church, but acknowledged. Members of the Church are made to understand from the beginning that their subjection to " powers " (ἐξουσίαι) which have authority over them, rests on divine ordinance. They must give them due obedience (Rom. xiii. 1 f.). They must render unto Cæsar the things which are Cæsar's (Matt. xxii. 21). They must pray for all that are in authority over them (1 Tim. ii. 1 f.). But from all these fellowships the Church is *distinguished*. It is the *communio s a n c t o r u m*. It stands or falls with none of the various forms and aims of these other fellowships. It is not confined within their boundaries and not involved in their mutual oppositions. Its own frontiers run right through the provinces of these other fellowships. Within the framework of these other fellowships in which it exists, and in face of the various interests by which these fellowships are animated, it has its own interest which is ever and everywhere the same. That is what the predicate *catholica* throws into special prominence. No tie to a people, a state, a culture must ever cause the Church to forget this *catholica*. It is *sancta*, it is even *ecclesia*, only where it is in essence and in will decisively *catholica*. Everything else that it is possible for it to be and will, comes fundamentally and can only come after that. Whether it is, as an organisation, " People's Church," National Church, State Church or else Free Church—all that is, it may also be observed, a question of secondary importance. In both forms it may or may not be catholic and therefore holy Church. The only question *seriously* put to it is, whether it is *catholic* and therefore *holy* Church, *communio sanctorum*.

In what follows we speak of the Church's foundation and of its government, of its commission and of its life, of its frontiers and of its aim.

1. The Church's *foundation* at once implies its *government :* that is the first point where the holiness and catholicity of the Church have to be made manifest. It is not as if the Church had somehow and somewhere been " instituted," and then the problem, Who rules the Church ? could crop up as a second problem, shall we say the practical problem ? But the very foundation of the Church is also the installation of its government, and wherever in the field of practice questions are asked about Church government, reference must be made instantly and seriously to its foundation. But the foundation of the Church is the outpouring of the Holy Spirit upon the apostles at Pentecost, which again consists in this : that the work of the Son of God accomplished on Good Friday and revealed on Easter day became present to these men in such a way that, as Gospel for themselves and others, it became their very

own concern, the truth by which they lived and which they were thereby commissioned to proclaim. The Church was not founded as the result of a human intuition or in consequence of a human resolution. Neither the genius of individuals, nor the instinct or the enthusiasm of a crowd created it. No one was asked whether he wanted something in the nature of the Church. No one was endowed with the skill to build it. No one was worthy, yes, no one was not unworthy, to set his hand to this task. An Apostle is made, as Paul writes (Gal. i. 1), " not of men, neither by man, but by Jesus Christ, and God, the Father, Who raised Him from the dead ". It is the act of the exalted Jesus Christ Who gave Himself to His own by giving to them His Spirit, that makes the Church a fact, an event, amongst men, that makes it an event in the shape of a human assembly and community, of a place in the human scene, formed and staged by men, a piece of human history. But it is just in this event which founded the Church that He still rules the Church. Without doubt this act cannot by any means become a thing of the past. There could be no room for a government of the Church after or alongside of this act ; such a government would be meaningless. He, Jesus Christ, rules the Church, and none beside Him. Neither can the assembly and community rule itself—the democratic misunderstanding of the Church !—nor can it be ruled by an official or by a number of officials—the monarchic aristocratic misunderstanding ! Since man has not created and founded the Church, he cannot be its Lord. It does not belong to him ; it belongs neither to the crowd nor to any deputy of this crowd, nor to the religious genius who, with or without official status, happens to come to the front out of the crowd. No one should want to be called Rabbi, Father, Leader (*Führer*) in the Church : " One is your Leader, even *Christ*. . . . He that is greatest among *you* shall be your *servant* " (Matt. xxiii. 8 f.). To rule, to make war, to conquer, to conclude peace, to exercise authority, to make decisions, to lead the way—in the Church that can be the business of none other than the Word of God Himself, Who by becoming flesh chose, called and received all who believe in Him into unity with Himself, the Crucified and Risen One, Who reconciled them with God and in Himself brought their new life to light. How should those who do not even have an independent existence alongside of Him, get an independent sovereignty or even only a co-sovereignty in the Church ? In what sense should the limbs rule alongside of the Head—the earthly limbs alongside of the heavenly Head ? No, here it is a case of absolute sovereignty. Only with regard to the manner in which it is exercised is there need to explain that it is no longer the same as it was before the Ascension, nor yet the same as it will be after His Second Coming. The Church is indeed the Kingdom of God in the interim period. One can bluntly assert that, in founding the Church, Christ founds this interim period as proof of divine patience. The Church is the place given us for repentance, for conversion, for faith. It is perhaps of the Church in this, its interim state, that we are to think in regard to those " forecourts " in which a day is better than a thousand (Ps. lxxxiv. 10). And now it is of consequence that the foundation of the Church consists concretely in the foundation of the New Testament *apostolate* and in the retrospective legitimation of Old Testament *prophecy*. The Holy Spirit, through Whose

descent the Church was created was *in concreto* the
" Spirit of the *first* witnesses " and we have no reason
for maintaining that there has been any change since
then and that He has, as Schleiermacher fancied, trans-
formed Himself into a general Christian spirit. Under
this pretext it has happened again and again that, while
loudly extolling Jesus Christ and His grace, the Christian
has made himself lord of the Christian Church. Where
he does not aim at that, where he is prepared to let
Jesus Christ be Lord of the Church, there in act and fact
he allows the prophetic apostolic *Scriptures* to be master.
The Christ Who has absolute sovereignty in the Church,
and therefore in the time between the Ascension and the
Second Coming, is Christ in this concrete form which
He has given Himself. *He* rules, but He rules in the
concrete form of the *witness* to Him in the Holy Scriptures.
It is on that account that the Church is to be understood
as a *place*. It is the place that has the Biblical witness
for its boundary, the place in which Christ is proclaimed
and perceived under the direction of this *witness*, the
place in which it is this *witness* that has right and power,
victory and sovereignty. The Roman Catholic tradition
principle, and no less the New-Protestant doctrine of
the revelation of God in history imply inadmissible
invasions of the kingly office of Christ. They are due to
failure to recognise the time of the Church as an interim
period, as a time accordingly concretely limited, and
thus as the time to which the rule applies, " *He* that
heareth *you*, heareth Me " (Luke x. 16).

2. Having dealt with this fundamental article of the
doctrine of the Church, we have the field clear for the
second proof of the Church's holiness and catholicity
which consists in this : that its *commission* and its

life are not two different things but one. The Church is not an establishment and institution and then possibly in addition *communio sanctorum.* On the contrary, in being the former, it is the latter, and where it is not the latter it is assuredly not the former either. It is not a case of its having a commission, in order then (alongside of that) to have its own Church life. Rather its commission is also immediately its life. This, too, is to be understood on the basis of Christology. There we had the eternal Word's sovereignty over that human nature which exists solely in *Him,* exists therefore solely *in dependence* on Him ; and now here, corresponding to that, we have the sovereign superiority of the divine commission to the human life of the Church, which life is conditioned by Him to the uttermost. If this correspondence is a fact, that is, if the Church is really in that fundamentally subordinate position of the limbs of a body to its head, then its very existence consists in its subjection to Christ's commission and so in its execution of that commission. Both according to the express declaration (Matt. xxviii. 18 f.), and according to what we can learn from the New Testament about the actual practice of the Apostles, this commission consists in witnessing by means of the *preaching of the Gospel* and the *administration of the Sacraments.* No third action has a place beside these two, which are in essence one, the *ministerium verbi divini.* The saying about the keys of the Kingdom of heaven (Matt. xvi. 19) in particular must not be regarded as an extension but as another way of describing this one office and commission of the Church. It is in the reception and in the exercise of this one commission, and not otherwise, that the Church is *communio sanctorum, congregatio fidelium.* Over against this one commission neither pastoral work, nor social service, nor co-operation in the tasks of culture or of politics can claim an independent position and dignity. They are necessary and legitimate in the measure in which they are to be understood as special forms of the execution of this one commission. Christian parties ? Christian newspapers ? Christian philosophy ? Christian Universities ? The question must be very seriously asked whether such undertakings are in this sense necessary and legitimate. It is not out of resignation that reserve is enjoined at this point. It is not because the Church could be content to exist in a " corner of private piety ". No, but it is out of *respect* for that command, by which the Church stands or falls and which it has no business arbitrarily to improve on and exceed. It is out of *confidence* in the *worth* and relevancy of this command, it is out of the firm *assurance* that by pure proclamation and by the proper administration of the sacraments more is achieved and better results are obtained in the solution of just these pressing problems of life than by the best-intentioned measures for aid, action and enlightenment, that involve our stepping outside of the bounds of this small but mighty domain. This domain is marked off for us with the utmost exactness by the Ascension and by the Baptism on the one side, and on the other by Holy Communion and the Second Coming. It is a domain which has certainly a wealth of problems and tasks. By confining itself to this, its own domain, the Church will show itself as Master ; either that or not at all.

But now the positive side must be stated, namely, that the Church in its life may and should allow itself actually to draw courage from its commission, allow itself therefore to be directed by it, led by it, fashioned by it. I can do no more than touch on the things that fall to be considered here. The Church that lives by and in its commission will see to its own discipline and *order.* This order, however, will not be one that has been arbitrarily devised, but one that carries with it the performance of its commission. Therefore it will not rob ecclesiastical office of its dignity by understanding it as the exercise of the service that belongs to the whole community. And it will not do violence to the immediacy of the relations of the community to its Lord by recognising some of its members as separated for the exercise of this service. It will, of necessity, respect, seek and find the unity of the Church by keeping itself open for the apprehensions and experiences, for the advice and help of other Churches that recognise the same commission, and by striving to speak and to act in common with them. In relation to the world and to the error within its own ranks it will necessarily be a *confessing* Church, making its confession along with the fathers in the faith, but, for the very reason that it confesses with them, making its own confession and that also in the present. In other words, in obedience to its Lord and therefore in obedience to the Scriptures, it answers clearly and consistently and fearlessly the questions put to it from moment to moment. It will necessarily be a *missionary* Church, that is, it will not exist only for " Christians," and therefore, so to speak, only for its own sake, but in existing for Christians, it will at the same time exist for the " heathen," it will exist for the sake of the world reconciled in Christ to God. How would it be living in its commission if by its commission it were not mightily constrained so to do ? What does " living " Church mean ? Beware of all arbitrary ideas. Living Church can only mean, a

Church that lives by its *faith* and therefore by its *commission !*

3. The third proof of the holiness and catholicity of the Church consists in its being ready to acquiesce in recognising the *aim* of its existence in its very *limitation.* Here, too, there must be no abstraction. Any separation of limitation and aim in the Church—as if by limitation we were to understand its earthly human incompleteness, and by aim, its ideal existence—would undoubtedly mean the inner disintegration of the Church itself. The Church has its aim just where its limitation is. In this sense the familiar saying is right, that the Church exists to make itself superfluous and to abolish itself. This we can understand if we look at it from three points of view :—

(*a*) We know the Church, so far as its form is concerned, only as the totality of those who are its members by *outward* confession. The conditions of this outward confession can be made as strict as possible, in order to ascertain whose confession is a real confession of faith, regarded and accepted by God as real, yet without its being possible in this way to ascertain the *corpus* or the *societas electorum.* The *true* Church in this sense, that is, the true statistics of those who are members of the body of Christ, will always be known only to God. Divine election is the limit of the Church that we know, the *ecclesia visibilis.* But just this limit is its aim. It is this limit that is meant when we confess *credo ecclesiam.* In doing that, we do not look out beyond the Church that is known to us, therefore beyond the visible Church, to some *civitas platonica.* For the visible Church is called just to be *societas electorum.* It is as such that, in unreserved trust in the promise made to it, it may and

146

should proclaim and hear the Gospel. God is Judge of the Church also, yes, particularly of the Church, but God in *Jesus Christ*, and so that God who to sinners is *gracious*. Neither with apprehension nor with arbitrary anticipation of His judgment has the Church to look forward to this Judge and to go to meet Him, but in completest confidence in the victory of *grace*.

(*b*) We know the Church only in its *disrupted* state, that is, we always know it only in the form of the denomination in which we are baptised and reared. There are other Churches beside the Reformed Church in which *we* must recognise the one true Church of Jesus Christ. Among these other Churches there are some, such as the Lutheran, in whose different confession we recognise again our own faith and therefore the one Church of Jesus Christ, just as members of the one family recognise each other as offspring of one progenitor. There are other Churches, such as that of Roman Catholicism or, within the Evangelical Church itself, the synagogue of New-Protestantism, in whose confession we are *not* able to recognise our own faith and therefore the one true Church of Jesus Christ, and which we must with heavy hearts *repudiate* as a false Church. Yet we ourselves should not be in the Church of Jesus Christ if we were not prepared right in view of this *limitation* of the Church to confess in the words of Eph. iv. 4 f., " *One* body and *one* spirit, even as also ye were called in *one* hope of your calling ; *one* Lord, *one* faith, *one* baptism, *one* God and Father of us *all*, Who is *over* you *all* and *through* you *all* and *in* you *all* ". We know only too well, and we know not at all what we are thereby saying. Loyalty to the same Lord holds us firmly to the limit and points us over that to the aim of the Church. The

147

aim, the one Church of Jesus Christ, is precisely there where now we see the boundary, where for the sake of faith, of love and of hope, we must see it, and thus may neither overlook it nor even overstep it.

(*c*) We know the Church only in its *unlikeness* to the Kingdom of God. The Church is, as we saw, directly constituted by the fact that the Kingdom of God has come near in the Epiphany of Jesus Christ, but only near, and that we still live in time, which is not eternity. The phenomenon of the hiddenness of the body of Christ and the phenomenon of the disunity of the one Church bring that fact very clearly before our eyes. But it did not need even that to make this plain. Why only sermon and sacrament? Why only confession and order? Why only office and congregation? Why only faith and obedience? Why only memory and expectation? Why only confessional Church? Why, in a word, only Church and not Kingdom of God? Why not God all in all? All the fanatics of all the ages have hammered at these closed doors and—the Church would be ill-advised if it failed to do it *along with* them, if it could rest content with being " only " Church. Nay, in its whole activity it must be looking out to this its boundary. It must pray and cry, Thy Kingdom come!—in other words, be a waiting and a forward-hastening Church. Here it really stands before its aim. But in contrast to the fanatics it will keep reminding itself that its very aim is also its limit. When the Kingdom of God has come, the Church will no more exist. As long as the Church exists, the Kingdom of God must be its boundary. And as long as the Kingdom of God is its boundary, it can and must, with all that belongs to it, reconcile itself to be merely Church. Only the arrogance of a religious or moral enthusiasm could want to overlook or over-run that limit. Faith acknowledges it while believing in its future abolition. The hope of the Church is a living but at the same time also a bridled hope.

That is a very short account of the fundamental laws of the *sancta ecclesia catholica*, of the *communio sanctorum*.

XV

REMISSIONEM PECCATORUM

WE all know questions 59-64 of the Heidelberg Catechism in which, with reference to the explanation already given of the whole symbol, the question is raised: "But what does it help you now that you believe all this," and then is answered, in common with Calvin's Catechism, by the development of the doctrine of the justification of the sinner before God only by faith in the satisfaction, righteousness and holiness of Christ granted and imputed to us by grace. In this answer, so characteristic of the whole Reformation of the sixteenth century, are we to see an illegitimate narrowing down of the Biblical message? The Apostles' Creed at any rate answers, No. For at that very point amongst its clauses where the question might be raised, "What now does it mean for man to be awakened to faith by the Holy Spirit, and to become a member of the Holy Catholic Church?" it gives the answer—to use again the words of Luther's Catechism: ". . . in which Christian Church He daily *forgives* richly all my *sins* and those of all believers". The answer to the question, what man obtains from receiving the Holy Spirit and being in the Church is *remissionem peccatorum*. Manifestly according to this old and possibly primitive document, everything else that might here be named must be subordinated to that one fact, must be understood by that one fact. Therefore judged at any rate by the standard of the Apostolicum, the Reformation understood the Biblical message aright when it conceived the practical scope of the creed to be, that by faith we receive forgiveness of sins.

Let us imagine for a moment that something else stood here. Why should that not be the case? Would it have surprised anyone if the first centuries of the Church had described the benefit of salvation that faith brought to a man as the new law, or as true knowledge of God and of His mysteries, or as sacramental communion with the Deity, or as the true repose of the soul in Christ or in the Spirit? Of moralism, Gnostic intellectualism, pietism and mysticism there was already at that date more than sufficient. And how much more appealing the Apostolicum could be to modern consciousness, if at this place, instead of forgiveness of sins, the theme were personal conversion and renovation of life, or the renovation of human society, or the knowledge of higher worlds, or of heroic piety. And since it is possible to get a good, even in part a very good, indeed Biblical, meaning for all these things, what should prevent their being actually mentioned here? Certainly our whole exposition of the Credo would have had to be quite different, if one of these other things had actually been named here. We should not then have dared to put the second article into the middle of the whole in the way in which that has been done, and we should not have dared to regard it, and therefore the reality of the divine revelation, so definitely from the point of view of the reconciliation of sinful man. We should not then have ventured to treat so emphatically the reality and the action of the triune God as the proper object of faith, and we should not then have ventured to emphasise so strongly again and again the idea of God's free grace as the real meaning and key to all those mysteries of faith here set before us. No one who, in thinking of what is received and possessed in Christian faith, had really one of these other things in his eye, could have followed the course of these Lectures up to now without conscious or unconscious opposition. But would this opposition of his not properly have to be directed also— quite apart from this passage—against all the rest of the symbol text ? Does not this text itself—quite apart from any exposition here given—run in a direction that makes it impossible to regard the new law as equally suitable in this passage, or the peace of the soul or social renovation or any of those other things that might have stood here ? It is not we who have placed this second article so dominatingly right in the centre of the symbol and who have assigned this dominating position within the second article itself to the Cross of Christ. It is not we who have given the symbol the form that makes it predominantly the confession of God, Father, Son and Holy Spirit, and that makes all its other statements into predicates of this subject. It is not we who have so arranged that the activity of the triune God, as here described, appears at all decisive points as that inconceivable mystery of divine condescension and compassion. The content of the symbol itself forced the theological exposition to take fundamentally just the direction that we have taken. But if that is so, then it will follow understandably and as a matter of course that the theme at this point should necessarily be—the forgiveness of sins.

If we may assume that that happens with a certain inner necessity, this is not to say that all those other things, interpretable in a good and serious sense and even in accord with the guidance of Holy Scripture itself, are simply struck out and repudiated by the Creed. It is only said that not in any circumstances does anything come before this, and that it is in relation to this, in its position of primacy, that everything else is to be understood and also tested as to whether it had not about it perhaps more of the nature of human ideals and therefore of the nature of our sinful flesh, than of the nature of a gift of the Holy Spirit. Some of them, when subjected to this test, we shall venture in this connection to speak of only in an undertone, others perhaps not at all. For the Creed certainly says that forgiveness of sins or justification of the sinner by faith is *the* gift of the Holy Spirit by which all others, so far as they are really that, must submit to be measured ; that it is the common denominator, so to speak, upon which everything that can seriously be called Christian life must be set. The Creed assuredly rejects that view which would place forgiveness of sins as a good thing for Christian faith alongside of many others. No, says the Creed, grace means forgiveness of sins. And to receive grace means to receive forgiveness of sins. No doubt we shall have to reflect that, on the Biblical view, that means more than at a first glance would appear from the wording. But we must not depart from this strict conception of " grace ". Only in so far as it is forgiveness of sins through the Gospel is it regeneration also, and conversion and establishment of the law (Rom. iii. 31) and therefore sanctification, gift of knowledge, gift of repentance and of obedience, gift of love, of patience and of hope, source and sum of really good works, a candle set in a candlestick, giving light to all that are in the house (Matt. v. 15). Everything, absolutely everything and to the last degree, is determined and conditioned by the fact that forgiveness of sins is gifted to man and received by him as a gift. Without that, everything else is Jewish

153

morality or heathen idealism and in one way or another demonic magic, which, whatever the lustre of virtue and devotion and brotherliness it may invest itself with, does not help man but rather ruins him. Grace is forgiveness of sins. " From this article there can be no budging nor slackening, though heaven fall and earth and all else besides " (Luther).

In order to understand this hard point, that grace is forgiveness of sins, we must start out from an equally hard statement in our last Lecture but one. " The Holy Spirit," we there asserted, " is the Spirit of the *Word* of God, the Spirit of *Jesus Christ.*" This statement means practically that to the man who receives the Holy Spirit and so is awakened to faith and so becomes a member of the Holy Catholic Church, it becomes *manifest* that the work which the *Word of God* accomplished in the flesh— that change from judgment to grace, from death to life in the cross and resurrection of *Christ*, which in its entirety we have described as the work of reconciliation—was accomplished in the flesh, in the humanity, in the human nature of this Other—because this Other is the Son of God—for *him himself* and therefore *in him himself.* Christ is not far away from the man who receives the Holy Spirit and who therefore is awakened to faith, but is near to him, and he is not far from, but is near to, Christ. He is no longer separated from Christ but is spiritually united with Him, namely, with His flesh. He has heard the Word of God spoken to him and so has made it his own. As the sign of Holy Communion testifies and confirms, he has spiritually eaten His body and drunk His blood. Therefore his own flesh has in faith become partaker of the flesh of the Son of God. The humanity of the Son of God has become present in faith to him in his own humanity. The humanity of the *Son of God !* That must mean first of all that by this appropriation and representation we do not become the lords of Christ, but that by it, He becomes *our* Lord, we are brought before Him, He makes *us* His own, His own in the way in which His, the Son of God's, own flesh is His own, namely, in absolute superiority, so that our own life in the flesh has ceased to be our own, so that He Who lives in us is *Christ*, the Son of God, while our life is nothing but the life of faith in Him (Gal. ii. 20).

But that implies that what He did in His flesh was done *for us* and therefore *in us*. The only thing that could stand in the way of this would be the separation, the difference between our life in the flesh and that of the Son of God. If this separation continued, then we should be and continue our own lords ; and as our own lords we should not even conceive what He did in His flesh, much less let it be done both for us and in us. But this very separation and difference are, even in time, abolished in our election by free grace from all eternity, and in our calling to faith by the Holy Spirit, hidden as that may be and may remain to us. The revelation of the Spirit as the miracle of hearing the Word of God reveals and convinces us that we are one with Him, not outside of, but " in Christ," " members of His body, of His flesh and of His bones " (Eph. v. 30), and therefore that all that He did was done both for us and in us. Therefore, that actually *we*, as sinners, are crucified, dead and brought to the grave in and with His flesh, and that actually we, clothed with the righteousness of obedience which He manifested in His flesh, are raised from the dead in and with His flesh. That we are taken *with* Him on that way of His, in which He suffered, died and is risen. That all this, however hidden, is as true *for us* as for Him Himself, that, consequently, everything happened *in us* too—that is what is made clear to us in faith and therefore by the Holy Spirit.

And if we are again to ask what it means for us, what benefit it is to us that we believe, that is, that our " being in Christ " becomes manifest to us, and that therefore the death and resurrection of Christ benefit us—then we can and must certainly give the preliminary and correct general answer, that this means our regeneration and conversion and the establishment of the law of God, means the *sanctification* of our life in the flesh. How could I fail to feel myself almost literally lifted up by the hair of my head when I hear, as the Heidelberg Catechism puts it summarily in Question 1, " that I, with body and soul, both in life and in death, am not my own, but belong to my faithful Saviour Jesus Christ " ? What is all moral and religious enthusiasm beside the fundamental change that breaks into the life of man, with this knowledge of his being carried along with Christ upon this way and therefore of his being object of this adoption, expropriation and appropriation ? Now he will surely know what *faith* means, now seeing he knows that it is only in faith in the Son of God that he has his *life* at all. But now he will see this life of his as a life in the *flesh* that he can only spend as life of faith now and as long as it lasts, as life in *repentance*, in a daily dying of the old man, in a daily resurrection of the new. Now the *commandments* of God show him the just wrath he has escaped, but they show him also the way of gratitude on which he now has timidly yet obediently to set foot. Now, no longer lord of himself, he has become free for service of his brothers, in whom Christ meets him with the reminder that everything we do, or fail to do, to them is done, or not done, to

Him Himself. And now he becomes at once a happy man and a man disquieted in the highest degree, at once a man of peace and a fighter hard as iron, a man who lives in the complete freedom of the children of God, and who just as such is held in discipline, full of hope and just as full of patience, watching and praying, zealous for the House of God and glowing with love, and, with all that, resigning everything, absolutely everything, to the Lord Himself, a humble man, not only " in heart " but *de facto* and just as such a messenger of God's glory. But how could we think even here to get a glimpse from afar of completeness ? Even Calvin in his famous chapter *de vita hominis Christiani* was able in the last resort to speak of this sanctification only in hints and in accordance with the measure of his own ideas.

We might go on the whole day long speaking ever so beautifully and profoundly, with ever so much knowledge of life and ever so Scripturally, yet we should be speaking into the air if we did not make clear to ourselves that, with the *vita hominis Christiani* just as with the *vita hominis pagani*, it would be mere pretence and deception, were the decisive content and meaning of the union between Christ and us, and therefore the decisive content of revelation and faith not the *forgiveness of sins*, the *justification* which we receive by faith alone. If sanctification is taken seriously, that is, as meaning that in faith we are subjected to the law of Christ, and if, further, we have the idea that it is possible for us to satisfy with our Christian life Christ's claim upon us, then there is no concealing from us that we never maintain ourselves before the law of Christ, that the loveliest, boldest, even most Biblical description of the Christian life can do no more than shame us, sadden us and make us doubtful whether we are Christians, not to speak of our doubts about the Church as the communion of saints. His claim, our sanctification through Him, must logically mean that we are set apart and claimed by Him for God, that we stand in the sight of God just as righteous, just as serviceable, just as obedient as He Himself in the days of His flesh. Now in *our* Christian life, as surely as it is still a life in the flesh, there can be absolutely no talk of such a thing. Our faith, our repentance, our obedience, our brotherly love, our patience and our zeal, our watching and praying—all these as *our* work, as *our* accomplishment and exhibition cannot suffice to display our righteousness before God. Their insufficiency is not only in part, not only quantitative, but *fundamental* and *qualitative*. Just the Christian man and therefore, be it noted, just the sanctified, only the sanctified, man will acknowledge and confess himself—that is, himself in so far as, even if in faith, he yet lives *his* life—as a sinner before God ; a sinner, whose very sanctification, since it could only hand him over to despair or to frivolity, would have to grow into curse and perdition, were it not its innermost nature that that unfathomable change, which the Son of God makes *in* His own, consists in something He does *for them*, does *in their place*. *Everything* that we have said about the Christian life and that could be said is *true* and *valid*, but the strength of the truth and validity does not lie in any Christian life, not even in that of the most Christian man, embracing with the utmost seriousness every conceivable rule and principle of this life, nay, but solely in the Son of God Himself, faith in Whom is the meaning of this life. We see here concretely once

more the significance of the interim period between
Ascension and Second Advent and understand why we
are exhorted now : Seek those things which are above,
where *Christ* is ! Why ? Because in this interim period
it is only the fact that we are forgiven and will be forgiven again and again that enables us to live. Forgiveness, however, means this : that Christ takes our place.
Christianity does not exist for a moment or in any respect
apart from Christ. He sanctifies us and it is to bliss
and not to perdition that faith in Him sanctifies, because
He has fulfilled the claim made upon us and because
in faith in Him we can and should be completely and
absolutely satisfied and content that *He* has fulfilled that
claim, and can and should greet that fact with warmth
and confidence. Our faith, if it is proper faith, is completely and entirely our adjustment towards this He !
If it is that, then our Christian life is neither pretence
nor delusion.

In its determinative content that faith, which is the
secret of the Christian life, means giving ear to the
commanding question, " How art thou righteous before
God ? " and to the answer which is given to this question
(Heidelberg Catechism, Q. 60) : " Only by true faith in
Jesus Christ : that is, although my conscience accuse
me that I have grievously sinned against all the commandments of God, and have never kept any of them
and that I am still prone always to all evil, *yet* God,
without any merit of mine, of mere grace, grants and
imputes to me the perfect satisfaction, righteousness
and holiness of Christ, as if I had never committed nor
had any sin, and had myself accomplished all the
obedience which Christ has fulfilled for me, if only I
accept such benefit with a believing heart ". I should

like to add to this passage from the Heidelberg Catechism the following question and answer from the
Catechism of H. F. Kohlbrügge : " To what little word
may you cling when you fail to find in yourself a single
sign of true grace, and are on that account grievously
cast down ?—To the little word ' Yet ' ! " In point of
fact, the pith and substance of faith in the forgiveness
of sins consists in holding on to this " yet " in view of
Jesus Christ as the One Who claims us by taking our
place and Who therefore claims us in free grace. That
is the pith and substance of faith in the forgiveness of
sins and so of Christian faith and so also of the whole
of the *vita hominis christiani.*

XVI

CARNIS RESURRECTIONEM, VITAM AETERNAM. AMEN

IF there is a holy catholic Church and therefore an assembly, a place, a community in which forgiveness of sins for Christ's sake is proclaimed to man, and if the existence of the Church and this proclamation that is made in it are the work of the Holy Spirit and therefore of God Himself, then that means : in the midst of human history and society, in the midst of this all-too-familiar world and time, in the midst of the environment of human existence, the nature of which each in some measure realises best from his own nature, there is sent forth here with the whole force of divine truth a *promise*, a *hope*. It is not possible to receive the Holy Spirit, it is therefore not possible to be in the Church and for Christ's sake obtain forgiveness of sins, without thereby participating also (and that with equal certainty and necessity) in this promise and hope. It is of this promise and hope that the conclusion of the creed speaks : *Carnis resurrectionem, vitam aeternam !* That assuredly means : over against human history and society, time and world, there is a totally different future existence of man. Man as he is to his own self-knowledge has a reflection of himself held up in front of him in which he appears as a completely new man. And he now hears this reflection saying to him : You who here and now are *this*, will then and there be *that*. Your membership of the Church and the forgiveness of your sins for Christ's sake would only be a sham if you did not have standing before you in the same power and truth this future existence of yours. Your confession of God the Holy Spirit and so your *credo in Deum* generally would have their seriousness put in doubt if you were suddenly to come to a stop here and refused to go on. The future being of the *credentes,* the resurrection of the flesh and eternal life, were certainly spoken of secretly (here and there even very openly) from the first clause of the Credo onwards. But it is now, only now, that, seeing this also has been *expressly* and *specially* set forth as an integral part of Christian knowledge, there can be said, *Amen,* That is true ! " Now faith is an assurance of things hoped for, a certainty of things not seen " (Heb. xi. 1). If the whole vigour and sublimity of the Christian Credo is to stand unequivocally before our eyes, then there is real need of expressly and specially enforcing the fact that, *along with* God, Father, Son and Holy Spirit, *we ourselves* in *this* sense are object of faith.

This last word of the Credo is concerned with the enforcing, emphasising and unfolding of truth already perceived and known. About what happens to man on the basis of the reconciliation accomplished in Christ we can at bottom say no more and nothing else than, *credo in Spiritum sanctum, credo ecclesiam, credo remissionem peccatorum.* It is not possible for us to believe or proclaim anything more or anything in any way better than that. So-called Eschatology can do no more than display and develop in a quite definite way how all that, and so how all the rest of the Creed, is meant as confession of the promise given to man, of the hope set up before him. It is easy to

162

understand how Eschatology could play such a comparatively insignificant rôle in the theology of the Reformers. They knew how to make so much of forgiveness of sins in particular that to them and their contemporaries anything of decisive importance that is to be said about the resurrection of the flesh and eternal life could be taken as said under that head. Nevertheless, it can be described as a weakness of Reformation theology, a weakness which revenged itself later and has been doing so right up to our own day, that it did not follow more energetically than it did the direction the symbol gave on the firm basis of both Old and New Testaments, and repeat from the standpoint of the future all that has been said from the standpoint of the present. Without saying anything new, this last part of the symbol repeats what has gone before in such a new way that its character as revelation-truth, as article of faith, comes once again clearly into view. Faith in the Holy Spirit, in the Church, in the forgiveness of sins, includes in itself faith *not only* in God, *but also* in *man* in so far, but only in so far as, in it all and with it all, we believe in the resurrection of the flesh and in an eternal life, and as by " man " there is understood that reflection of his future being that is held in front of us—not the man we are, but the man that, by virtue of the promise and hope that are given to us, we shall be. *This* man has his place together with God (or really with Jesus Christ !) in the Credo.

After what has been said our best course in dealing expressly and specially with this promise and hope is to make our starting-point the three preceding articles : *credo in Spiritum sanctum, credo ecclesiam* and *credo remissionem peccatorum.* In these three points we have stressed with the utmost emphasis the fact that what is spoken of is the Spirit of *Jesus Christ*, the Church created, upheld and ruled by *Jesus Christ*, the forgiveness that is bestowed on us in *Jesus Christ*.   In saying that, we imply the highest degree of *unity* between Jesus Christ and His own, a unity that in itself is in its *substance* unsurpassable. Even in the present there is no defect in this unity.   We cannot go beyond having all things in Christ.   It is no abatement to have to say that we have everything *only* in Him, that in ourselves we are empty and futile, that without Him we should be lost, that that " yet " mentioned at the end of the last Lecture refers exclusively to Him and goes beyond being a vain boast and protestation only as related to Him.   Actually everything that had to be done for the reconciliation of man with God was, as we showed in its place, already accomplished in the death of Christ. There lacked only its disclosure ; for the divine act of reconciliation took place, not in the revelation of His glory, but in the concealment of His divine condescension. That then is what was accomplished in His resurrection from the dead.   And now when we speak of His unity with His own in the present and in the future, we are dealing with exactly the same concealment and dis-closure.   It is not that the unity is here smaller and there greater, but here it is concealed and there manifest.   The present is the ***regnum gratiae,*** between the Ascension and the Second Coming.   The future is the ***regnum gloriae*** set open by the Second Coming.   In its *form* the unity be-tween Christ and His own is at present such as is *not* able to continue, or is able to continue only as long as this time lasts ; but after that it must give place to *another* form.   The form of this unity here and now is this : that for the Church Jesus Christ is hidden with God in the same way as the Church itself is hidden in the world.   He is not im-

mediately present to His own nor therefore are His own
immediately recognisable either to others or to themselves.
On His side everything depends absolutely on the mission
and operation of His spirit and on our side absolutely on
faith.   Again, that does not mean any defect in this unity,
any diminution in its reality and so of the help, the consolation, the guidance which His own receive from Him.
Yet the form of this unity cries out for change, for resurrection.   Yes, it signifies in itself a question that is the
more real and burning because, while it clearly enough
contains its answer within itself, it has not by any means
so *received* that answer that as question it no longer exists
for us.   We " *have* " the Holy Spirit only in His fight
against the flesh, and especially in the fight of the flesh
against Him, and therefore strictly speaking always in the
prayer for Him that He Himself has put into our heart and
mouth.   The Church which we know is the Church which
is contending against the world on the one hand, and on the
other against error, temptation, apostasy in its own ever
so carefully closed ranks, and which as far as the eye can
reach is again and again failing in this fight and being
defeated.   And it is in this way that, since we receive forgiveness of sins, we are ourselves God's children and, according to 1 John iii. 2, it doth indeed not yet appear what
we shall be.   That is, we do not know ourselves as free of
sin.   It is only by recognising the boundlessness of our
sinfulness that we can boast of our righteousness.   In
other words, we can only obey in faith, i.e. only by our
faith in the obedience of Christ can we guarantee that any
action of ours has been or will be obedience.   Even as
iusti we are and we remain *p e c c a t o r e s.*   However certain
it may be in itself, faith is faced all along the line with the
plausible idea that it is only an aimless and groundless

venture, that by its own resources it stands and by itself it falls and is never—what it really is as faith in Jesus Christ—in itself certain and immovable. We have the treasure which is ours in " earthen vessels " (2 Cor. iv. 7). We have the promise and, in and with it, also most certainly the fulfilment, but the fulfilment only in the form of the promise that consoles us, that suffices us, and makes us confess that we are strangers and pilgrims on the earth (Heb. xi. 13). It is of the passing of this *form* of our unity with Jesus Christ that Holy Scripture speaks when it speaks of the *resurrection of the flesh.* And when it speaks of *eternal life* it is of the *new* form that it speaks, emerging into strength after this passing. It speaks of the carrying out of the accomplished reconciliation of man in his future *redemption.* It tells us that Easter and the forty days were not a miracle tossed down by chance into the midst of human history, but the sign of what shall come to pass and be at the final end as the aim and meaning of all history. It is the message of the Kingdom of God which has not only come near, but which, when all other kingdoms have been done away, is the one and eternal Kingdom.

Let us be clear that, when we say that, we are again speaking of the Second Coming of *Jesus Christ.* Christian Eschatology is different from all other expectations for the future, whether they be worldly or religious or religious-worldly, in that it is not primarily expectation of something, even if this something were called resurrection of the flesh and eternal life, but expectation of the *Lord.* *He* awakens the dead ; *He* gives eternal life ; *He* is the Redeemer, as certainly as redemption is the revelation of the reconciliation that took place in Him. Our joy at the coming change can only be the anticipation of the joy of

His marriage, at which we may be present. Everything depends upon its being *His* revelation that issues out of *His* concealment in the invisibility of God. The glory of human nature, the form of the second redeemed Adam that is at present so completely hidden even from the faith of His own, is real only in *His* person and is to be revealed in us only through an act of His person. What indeed is involved is that, as Head of His members, He draws us after Himself and to Himself—into the visibility of His own resurrection, into the harmony of His own exaltation. Hope of our resurrection and of eternal life is therefore nothing at all, if it is not primarily hope of Him, and not of Him as of the fulfiller of our wishes, but of Him Who carries out in us His *own divine* will. Therefore it cannot but be that in regard to its object hope is completely united with faith.

But the question mark set against this unity with Christ, in spite of its certainty, in its very certainty, the veil that makes it a unity which is hidden from us, is first of all and quite concretely the fact that even those who believe in Christ, and are on that account united with Him, must *die* just as if they too were " dead in trespasses and sins " (Eph. ii. 1). According to the New Testament their " falling asleep " (1 Thess. iv. 13 ; 1 Cor. xi. 30 ; xv. 6 ; 2 Pet. iii. 4) is to be conceived as something that is not at all natural but rather as something very astonishing. It is not to be overlooked that most of the New Testament miracles are in some sense signs directed against the power of *death*. Between the resurrection of Christ and the resurrection of His own there exists so intimate a connection that Paul (1 Cor. xv. 13, 16) must solemnly declare : " If the dead rise not, then is *not* Christ raised ". Unity with Him does *not* in that case

167

mean—being reconciled with God. "Your faith is vain,
ye are yet in your sins" (1 Cor. xv. 17). But even the
members of the body of Christ die and the resurrection
has not yet taken place. The life and immortality which
Jesus Christ has brought to light through the Gospel
(2 Tim. i. 10) do *not yet* mean that death has lost its power
over us also. We must still die. Tears will still be shed ;
still there will be no lack of sorrow, crying and pain ; the
former things are not yet passed away (Rev. xxi. 4).
Death as separation of the immortal soul from the mortal
body confirms the fact that we *still* exist in a state of
ambiguity as children of Adam and as children of God, as
righteous and as sinners, in the time of Pontius Pilate and
in the time of grace. This "not yet" and this "still"
constitute together the condition of φθορά, of corruption,
of weakness, of dishonour (1 Cor. xv. 42 f.) which certainly
does not diminish our unity with Christ here and now,
but without a doubt conceals it. We do indeed live with
Him and therefore "in eternal righteousness, innocence
and blessedness" (Luther), but it is in the teeth of the
sharpest opposition of our human-temporal existence that
we so live that existence which is not yet conformed to
human nature in Christ or is conformed only in faith ; it
is in the teeth of the opposition of the flesh. The self-
same man who in Christ is already here and now raised
high above all angels, still belongs in himself to the old
sin-ruined creation which sighs for redemption, and that
means, concretely, redemption from death. Even the
step from Rom. vii. to Rom. viii. does not do away with
that dualism which consists, on the one hand, in sins
having to be unveiled in believers, even in them, really in
them, by the law of God, and on the other hand in death's
having to be made fearful by the unveiled sin (1 Cor. xv.

56), so that their peace with God necessarily means at once a desperate conflict with themselves, an incessant watching and praying, and a restless pressing toward the mark.

The *resurrection of the flesh* of which the symbol speaks, is the abolition of this position which is ours amid that contradiction between the grace and the gracelessness of our own existence as such.   Resurrection of the flesh means that the question, " Who will separate us from the love of God ? "—which here and now is certainly not one for which we are at a loss to find an answer—ceases in any sense to be a question.   Resurrection of the flesh does not mean that the man ceases to be a man in order to become a god or angel, but that he may, according to 1 Cor. xv. 42 f., be a man in *incorruption, power* and *honour, redeemed* from that contradiction and so *redeemed* from the separation of body and soul by which this contradiction is sealed, and so in the totality of his human existence *awakened* from the dead.   Resurrection of the flesh means very simply that the man will be in himself what he already is in Christ, new creation (2 Cor. v. 17) ;   that the garment of unrighteousness drops away from him and the garment of righteousness which he has for long been wearing secretly becomes visible.   Resurrection of the flesh means therefore that our existence as *carnal* existence, our heaven and earth as theatre of *revolt*, our time as time of Pontius Pilate, will be dissolved and changed into an existence, into a heaven and earth, into a time, of *peace* with God without conflict, of that peace which, hidden from our eyes in the flesh of Christ, is already a reality.

If, finally, *eternal life* is the name given to this new form of our unity with Jesus Christ, we shall again have to be on our guard against all those abstractions which our philosophic arrogance delights in. When eternity of our life is spoken of in the Christian Creed, it does not mean a life of any super-temporal kind, or timelessness or infinite time. It does not even mean a life in any kind of carefully and boldly conceived perfection. Nor does eternity of our life mean that this life of ours is annihilated and its place taken by some other life in some other world, even if it be an eternal world. Finally, eternity of our life does not mean that our life becomes identical with the life of God. But eternal life in the sense of Holy Scripture is this life that is ours now in this world that now is, this life, still, as it has always been, distinguished from the life of God, since it is created, but now, as a life that has become *new* in an earth that has become *new* under a heaven that has become *new*,—life that has become new in its relation to God its Creator, Reconciler and Redeemer. Become new in this respect, that it is now no more a life differing within itself, as, on the one hand, our life in Christ and, on the other, as our own life, but now (let this " now " be emphasised) *at once as eternal life and as our own life*, a life which is reconciled with God and therefore righteous and holy. The old theologians described this life as a life in the contemplation (*visio*) of God as He *is*, and in love towards God (*fruitio*) as He *desires* to be loved. And our Reformed Fathers in particular have stressed the view that, as the consummation of God's dealings with us, there will necessarily be a life in which we shall give *God* the *glory*. *In eum finem rediturus est Christus, ut gloriosus sit in sanctis suis et admirabilis in credentibus* (Fr. Turrettini). To such a life in unbroken peace with God and in the uninterrupted glorification of God we may no doubt ascribe supertemporaneousness, timelessness or infinite time, if instead we do not prefer to make it very clear to ourselves that we, who must do our thinking from this time that is known to us, have not the slightest idea what we are saying when we talk either positively or negatively about the time of that God with Whom we shall live in unbroken peace in eternal life. We can spare ourselves many unnecessary pains (for this is really enough to satisfy us) if we hold fast to what is the decisive feature of eternal life : that it is eternal in its being lived in the unveiled light of God and in so far participating in God's own life.

I conclude with the reminder that all that, too, is governed by the term *credo*. That there is not only a resurrection to life, but also a resurrection to judgment, therefore not only an eternal life but also an eternal death, is something that stands in another book. The symbol has not spoken of it. It has only hinted at it with the *inde venturus est i u d i c a r e*. But there we saw that in faith it is possible only to *hope* for, only to look *forward* to Christ even as Judge, yes, just as Judge. The judgment that is the object of our *faith* is the decision of victorious grace after the time of contradiction in which we exist here and now. Strictly speaking, it is not possible to have *faith* in another decision than this. Strictly speaking, it is not possible to *proclaim* another one. The strength of Christian proclamation, and with it of Christian Dogmatics, stands or falls with their viewing man as " in Christ " and so reckoning him as God's, and so not reckoning with his persistence in unbelief, with his being eternally lost. But admittedly they cannot receive, amongst their propositions, the denial of this other possibility nor therefore the positive doctrine of the apocatastasis as the final redemption of all men. Thereby they would be disannulling the *credo* as the presupposition of every Christian confession. We said in our first Lecture, and we must repeat now as our final word : *credo* means decision. Faith and unbelief with all their implications are two distinct things. And behind faith and unbelief there stands a divine choice, there stand God's gracious freedom and free grace, to which we would under no circumstances dare dictate that without choice all men must be saved. Blessed *is* he who *believes*. Here, therefore, the question will have to be put very seriously, " Believest thou that ? " to which we may then answer, " Lord, I believe, help thou mine unbelief ! " It will assuredly be better to answer thus and only thus. But we shall not be able to hazard any other answer if the last word of our Christian knowledge is really to be *vita aeterna*.

APPENDIX

ANSWERS TO QUESTIONS

ON 5TH AND 6TH APRIL, 1935

(From a Shorthand Report)

ALLOW me at the outset to say a few personal words.

When I studied the eighteen letters I received and the seventy questions they contained, it became very clear to me that you and I are not standing quite upon the same ground, and that we ought to keep this in view, I when listening to your questions and you when listening to my answers. This difference is not an absolute one—there is no such thing among men. It is a relative difference of the *ground* on which we find ourselves and, as such, it has got to be constantly borne in mind. What unites us is the sharing of a strong interest in the theological and ecclesiastical question. What separates us relatively is the fact that I have spent the last fourteen years of my life in *Germany*. But you are living as Dutchmen in *Holland*. That is not unimportant.

I shall first of all tell you what, in contrast to the position from which I speak, seems to me specifically Dutch in the questions put to me. All your questions betray to some extent that you are still able to pursue theology in *comfort*, with a certain calmness and detachment in regard to its problems, such as we once knew in

Germany but to-day know no longer. Here the delectable possibility is still yours of actually standing *over against* theological matters, of observing them, of having them approach in themselves. And now this Professor has blown in from Germany and with regard to many matters has said something very definite in a somewhat *binding* fashion, and you from your situation—that became very clear in your letters—are making a more or less cautious *defensive* movement. You would prefer that all questions, or as many as possible should be left open. Though known as " head of the Dialectic Theology," I am not dialectic enough for you ! And further, you can still afford to cultivate certain favourite lines of thought ; you wish to have certain *specialities* substantiated, others rejected. A profusion of parties was evidently waiting to hear what I had to say to their special interests. From this point of view disappointment could not be avoided.—You must not take all this as criticism. It has been a great pleasure to me to see that it is still possible to have this kind of theology in the world of to-day, for I am convinced that there is need for theology of this type also, as may well be still the case here with you.

I come from a Church and I come from a faculty whose life outwardly and inwardly is very different from the life of your Church here—and of your faculty. Be clear about what has been happening during these last months in Germany and Bonn. . . . Where such things are possible a very different wind is blowing. And it is not as if these things began in Germany only some months ago ; actually they have been going on for years, and in their presuppositions properly speaking ever since the end of the War. . . . All this has in Germany been a challenge to the Church and to theology, has been and is a challenge to each individual theologian to make a stand, to decide, to confess.—When you look back over my Lectures or listen now to my answers to your questions, you must reflect that such is the situation from which I am speaking. This situation, this direct call from the exigency of life, from the affliction the Church in Germany is at this moment suffering, has naturally its good *and* its dangerous sides. But there is no denying that the situation of an *ecclesia militans* can show a closer kinship to the great times of the Church's past, to the times in which Church dogma arose. Quite a different inner attitude is involuntarily adopted to this dogma than will be adopted in a quiet ecclesiastical situation in which it is merely honoured and probably also criticised as legacy of a past that no longer exists.

Let these remarks be premised to show and explain in a friendly way how it is impossible for us to see *entirely* eye to eye. For the rest we are closely enough connected to *desire* to understand each other and to a large extent also to *be able* to do so.—And now to the answering of some (only some) of the many questions put to me. I am arranging them as far as possible according to subject.

I. DOGMATICS AND CATECHISM

Both Dogmatics and Catechism aim at being *instruction in Christian doctrine on the basis of Holy Scripture*. There is this to be said of their common task : it is necessarily " pastoral " and " critical " in *both* cases, and it will not do to assign to Dogmatics the critical task, and to the Catechism the pastoral. The aim of both can be comprehended in the conception of *pure doctrine*. *Doctrine*, for they are both pastoral; *pure* doctrine, for they have both to be critical. So in the early Church no fundamental distinction was drawn between the task of Dogmatics and the task of the Catechism. Cyrill of Jerusalem, Augustine's Enchiridion! What predilection has been shown for the Heidelberg Catechism as textbook for dogmatic lectures, while on the other hand the Dogmatic of the Reformation period, Calvin's *Institutio*, was a " catechetical " work, as the name states.

The real difference between Dogmatics and Catechism is, I fancy, best described by the conceptions, *investigation* and *instruction*. As in every science so here also the two are not to be distinguished in principle but only in practice. Dogmatics is Catechism for the *ecclesia docens*, that is, for those who are themselves later called to give instruction as " catechists ". Therefore Dogmatics is mainly concerned with thinking things out, with raising *questions*, with pushing on to answers. On the other hand, the Catechism is the Dogmatics of the *ecclesia audiens*, intended first of all for the young, but as is shown especially by the Catechism of the Reformation period, fully intended also, with its special emphasis on the formulation of *answers*, for the whole Church. Like the *ecclesia docens* and *audiens*, so also Dogmatics and Catechism are to be distinguished, not theoretically, but only *in actu*. Dogmatics has to keep in view the fact that there is a Catechism. On the other hand, the Catechism will only be of use in the hand of the teacher when this teacher is dogmatically instructed. From this standpoint I can also answer the additional, concretely framed question : In principle it must be possible and justifiable for Dogmatics to *question* even an answer of the Catechism.

176

II. DOGMATICS AND EXEGESIS

The Credo is subject to Scripture, and Dogmatics has therefore to be continually corrected by Exegesis. It comes under its control. So we must now of course acquaint ourselves with what is to be understood by *Exegesis*. The exegesis which is, if I may use the expression, pre-ordered to Dogmatics must be an attempt to understand Holy Scripture within the pale of the Church : it must therefore be *theological* exegesis. By that I mean an exposition and explanation which have before their eyes *that* question which is to be put to prophets and apostles : To what extent is there given to us, here in this text, witness to *God's Word* ? Theological exegesis is an exegesis which is carried out under a quite definite presupposition. This is, firstly, that the reader of the Old and New Testaments remembers that in this book the Church has up to now heard God's Word ; and secondly, that this reader or investigator reads in the expectation that he himself will also for his time hear God's Word. The place of theological exegesis lies right between this remembrance and this expectation, corresponding to the time of the Church between Christ's Ascension and Second Coming. Therefore, *that* exegesis which is *norm* for Dogmatics is not an exegesis that is without presuppositions. There is no such thing. The alleged freedom from presuppositions of which a certain Gnosis is accustomed to boast, simply means that yet *another* presupposition is being made. Concretely this means that God's revelation is not to be reckoned with, that on the contrary it is possible to adopt a *neutral* attitude to what this Scripture points to, just as it is possible to take up this attitude to other things. This neutrality, this unconcern about God's revelation, and therefore this " freedom from presuppositions " is a presupposition exactly like any other. As a matter of method we have to choose which of these presuppositions shall be valid and of course in the Church only one comes into consideration as significant and relevant. If there is a Church, then the canon is to be read in a way that corresponds to the Church, that is with that remembrance and that expectation which I have mentioned. Please take note that in all that I have said the pretentious word " *pneumatic* exegesis " has not passed my lips. I am perfectly satisfied with furthering a *theological* exegesis.—

Such theological exegesis is the criterion of all the propositions of Dogmatics. It goes without saying that it is also the criterion by which the Credo and all the historical Confessions of the Church are measured and will always have to be measured. Along the whole line of Dogmatics the Reformation Scripture-principle must fundamentally remain in force. If it should really come to pass that such a theological exegesis saw itself compelled to strike out certain parts of the Credo (Virgin Birth, Resurrection ?) effect would have to be given to this demand without more ado. But to strike out the resurrection of Christ from the Credo—that could only be the demand of a very *un*theological exegesis. A theological exegesis will at once admit that the **resurrexit tertia die** stands at the centre of the New Testament witness in such a way that it can be said : this witness stands or falls with this statement. Of Ascension and Virgin Birth a theological exegesis will certainly not say that they stand at the centre of the New Testament witness, but rather that they stand in a very remarkable way on its margin. Certainly the Virgin Birth is en-

178

compassed with noteworthy question marks, and Dogmatics in its treatment of it must keep that fact in view. With regard to my Lecture I hope that you remember not only *that* I took up on this point a positive position, but also *how* and in what connection (**res** and **signum**) I did this. I came to the position of holding fast to the Virgin Birth from having ascertained in the New Testament that here a kind of signal is given which to the early Church was at all events sufficiently important to be received into the Credo. In the sense in which I have here presented the doctrine of the Virgin Birth, I think I am able to justify it before the claims of a theological exegesis. Therefore I cannot accept the objection that I went wrong in theological exegesis, and I must put the counter-question, whether it is not rather an exegesis, which believes itself to be at liberty to strike out the Virgin Birth, that is to be described as an untheological exegesis ?

III. Dogmatics and Tradition

I seem in my Lectures to have aroused particular displeasure in regard to this complex of questions ! I do not know whether I can justify myself in your eyes, but I want to try to explain to you my attitude to this problem. By what critical standard is tradition to be measured ? By tradition is to be understood, let us say, the *sum total of the voices of the Fathers*. In no circumstances obviously can this choir of the voices of the early Church be regarded as a second source of revelation (so it is regarded in the Roman Catholic Church, where logically the *teaching office* comes to the front as third source of revelation). No ! must be said to that. The Tridentinum which recognised tradition as source of revelation in the same manner as Holy Scripture, and the Vaticanum with its dogma of the infallibility of the Pope, signify the self-apotheosis of the Church, which is one of the most serious and enormous errors of the Roman Catholic Church. In contrast to that the Reformation Scripture-principle placed the Church *permanently* under the authority of the prophetic-apostolic Bible-Word ; and it did that in the opinion that, in this human distinction between the Church and Holy Scripture as *teacher* of the Church, there is expressed the abiding, lasting difference between the *Lord* of the Church and the Church as the assembly of believers upon earth. This barrier between Scripture and Church which points like a sign to the barrier between the Church and its Lord, has in Roman Catholicism been overstepped. *Tradition is not revelation.*—But there is this to be said— and it is in consonance with the Fathers of the Early Church and of the Reformation—that in the Church there can never be any question of overleaping the centuries and immediately (each trusting to the sharpness of his eye and the openness of his heart) linking up with the Bible. That is the Biblicism that significantly appeared again and again in the eighteenth and nineteenth centuries with the idea that it is possible to dismiss with a lofty gesture Nicænum, Orthodoxy, Scholasticism, Church Fathers, Confessions and cling " to the Bible alone " ! I am thinking of G. Menken, J. T. Beck, Hofman of Erlangen, Adolf Schlatter, all, significantly, gifted men ! This proceeding that seems to maintain so logically the Scripture-principle, always—strange to say—meant the emergence of a richly modern theology ! For these determined " Biblicists " had their contemporary philosophy in their heads, took it with them to the Bible and so most certainly read themselves into the Bible no less than Church Fathers and Scholastics. They were no doubt free of Church dogma but not of their own dogmas and conceptions. Luther and Calvin did not go to work on the Bible in this way. Neither should we. It is in the *Church* that the Bible is read ; it is by the *Church* that the Bible is heard. That means that in reading the Bible we should also hear what the Church, the Church that is distinguished from my person, has up to now read and heard from the Bible. Are we at liberty to ignore all that ? Do the great teachers of the Church, do the Councils not possess a—certainly not heavenly—but, even so, earthly, human "authority" ? We should not be too ready to say, No. To my mind the whole question of tradition falls under the Fifth Commandment : Honour father and mother ! Certainly that is a limited authority ; we have to obey God more than father and mother. But we have also to obey father and mother. And so I should call to all those who get excited when they hear the words Orthodoxy, Council, Catechism : Dear friends, no excitement ! There is no question of bondage and constraint. It is merely that in the Church the same kind of obedience as, I hope, you pay to your father and mother, is demanded of you towards the Church's past, towards the " elders " of the Church. That is quite simply an *ordinance*. Most certainly we cannot make an absolute beginning with the year 1935, carry out, as it were, a *creatio ex nihilo !* In this obedience to the Church's past it is always possible to be a very *free* theologian. But it must be borne in mind that, as member of the Church, as belonging to the *congregatio fidelium*, one must not *speak* without having *heard*. The Reformers knew that. You are aware that, in the Confessions, they refer to the Councils of the

181

early Church, and there can be no question that, with regard also to the content of their teaching, they appealed to the verdicts made by the Church in past times. Would it be possible to understand the doctrine of justification without the Trinitarian and Christological dogma ?

And now I should just like to ask you : What do you really mean when you use the word " Orthodoxy " ? Some of the questions along this line struck me as being —a little old-fashioned. In Germany, too, we have had experience of it, of this bogey of the " free " theologian. But it is really a scarecrow, with which in Holland, too, some one should make off ! " Orthodoxy " means agreement with the Fathers and the Councils. As that it can never be an end in itself. Repristination is nonsense. But where " Orthodoxy " is rejected in that frightened way, the question arises whether this rejection does not spring from an " orthodoxy " of one's own, connected perhaps with certain modes of nineteenth and twentieth century thought which are quite capable of forming a dogma. This dogma also has got its Church—with many chapels !—but people are never actually told that their allegiance to this Church must be unconditional. If only they knew definitely that here, too, there is a binding tie, they might be disposed to let this " tie " to the Church's past remain in force as after all a quite respectable affair. The more one listens and breaks free from the illusion that the world began with oneself, the more will one discover that these Fathers *knew* something, and that the scorned " orthodox " writers of, say, the seventeenth century were theologians of *stature*. And it can even happen that alongside of them modern theological literature will be found a little insipid and a little tedious. You must make the experiment yourselves. I, too, was once liberal and know the charm !

Well, I have been asked about the standard by which tradition is to be measured. It cannot by any means be a matter of opening the gates wide and allowing whole wagon-loads of old doctrine to enter without discrimination ! The past, too, had its mixture of pure and impure doctrine. The norm that determines our choice is Holy Scripture. Holy Scripture is the object of our study, and at the same time the criterion of our study, of the Church's past. As I read the writings of the " Fathers," the witness of Holy Scripture stands continually before my eyes ; I accept what interprets this witness to me ; I reject what contradicts it. So a choice is actually made, certainly not a choice according to my individual taste, but according to my knowledge of Holy Scripture.

IV. Dogmatics and Philosophy

If we open our mouths, we find ourselves in the province of philosophy. The fact that this holds also for Christian preaching and Dogmatics reminds us of the " incarnation of the Word ". The rule for the theologian is : All things are lawful for me. For example, it is lawful for me—I am answering a question—to speak of " noetic " and " ontic ". All things are lawful for me, but nothing shall take me captive. Now what does it mean to allow oneself to be taken captive ? When we speak in human conceptions, and so in the conceptions of a definite philosophy, we are as theologians undertaking something that is very perilous. The conceptions, used so to speak only as forms, may well have already a definite content that cannot be escaped, and that on occasion leads the theologian into a train of thought that has nothing to do with what, as theologian, he has to say. The attempt has been made from time immemorial to find an exit out of this problem of theological terminology by setting up theology and philosophy in partnership. This drama was performed in the most varied styles. One proceeded to say that the philosophic conceptions to be employed would have first of all to be " clarified ! " thereby going on the assumption that there are two sources of revelation, reason and history on the one side, and Holy Scripture on the other. If this conception of the relationship of theology and philosophy is fundamentally wrong, then only one possible course remains, that I as theologian, having my language, whatever it may be, go up with that language to an object that meets me in the witness of Holy Scripture. In making this witness my own, I am not free of all philosophy, but at the same time I am not bound to a definite philosophy. All things are lawful for me, but nothing shall take me captive. It will be by my allowing my thought and my speech to be absolutely determined by my object that theological knowledge will be formed. The Word is not subjected to human presuppositions, but human presuppositions are subjected to the Word. Naturally these human presuppositions are not to be extinguished, but it is one thing to allow the *sarx* systematically to take up beforehand a fortified position in my *intelligentia* and quite another to allow the *causa divina* to decide over the *intelligentia.* It need not trouble us that the human presuppositions are always present, but what I must know as theologian is that it is not my job to make a synthesis but to go upon a *way* which leads from the matter that commands to the form that serves. It is by moving along this way that theological conceptions are genuinely formed. Even so, plenty of accidents will occur, but at bottom this indicates a course in which violence will be done neither to theology nor for that matter to philosophy. Practically it is inadvisable for the theologian to bind himself for too long a period or too much in principle to *any* conceptions. That is, it is inadvisable for him to anchor himself systematically to any technical terminology. You all know how readily we get fixed in this respect, and how easy it then is for certain ruts to appear, ruts in which our thoughts run and in so doing acquire a dead weight which in theology they must never have. To take an example, there reached me from your ranks the complaint that I no longer used the language of the " Epistle to the Romans ". On the contrary, you should be thankful that I no longer burden you with " void " (*Hohlraum*) and " death-line " (*Todeslinie*)! That served its day. To-day it would be confusing and wearisome if I were to continue with it. I profoundly hope that in five or ten years I shall be able to speak yet another language than I do to-day, and that then also I shall be *compelled* to speak it. I should therefore advise you to cease this lamentation. At that time my whole desire was really to elucidate Paul's Epistle to the Romans. That was done partly by means of a strange incrustation of Kantian-Platonic conceptions. I was *at liberty* then to use these conceptions, but if I were to be told to-day that I *had* to use them, I should say with decision, No.

Further, it is forced down my throat that the Dogmatic theologian is under the obligation to " justify " himself in his utterances before philosophy. To that my answer is likewise, No. Dogmatics has to justify itself only

185

before God in Jesus Christ; concretely, before Holy Scripture within the Church. Certainly it has also the responsibility of speaking so that it can be *understood*, but there is not the slightest chance that any philosophy could here step forth as norm. It is a misunderstanding to think that in the " Epistle to the Romans " I directed myself consciously in criticism against the thought of modern man. As modern man I attempted to submit myself to the word of Paul.—It cannot be otherwise than that Dogmatics runs counter to every philosophy no matter what form it may have assumed. In point of fact theology must oppose every kind of Realism and Idealism. For it the significance of all representations and all conceptions does not lie in the representations and conceptions themselves, but has its subsistence in God. All our activities of thinking and speaking can have only a secondary significance and, as activities of the creature, cannot possibly coincide with the truth of God that is the source of truth in the world. The value of what theology has to say is measured by no standard except that of its *object*. There is always the possibility that what is said may be " not understood "; that possibility cannot be excluded. Even Holy Scripture is very often not understood. But no philosophy can deliver the key to us. The question of the " proper " language of theology is *ultimately* to be answered only with prayer and the life of faith.

V. Exegesis and the Science of History

We have already spoken of the conception of *theological exegesis* which understands Scripture as witness of God's revelation, that is, as pointer to an actual event taking place in space and time, an event, however, which is based directly on the compassion of God Who wills to speak to us men and to have dealings with us men. The object of the Biblical witness is to be understood as such an event, an event that is *actual*, yet is *based* on the *compassion*, on the *will of God*. The two are not to be separated. There are, so to say, two planes that intersect. Biblical exegesis can fundamentally only be interpretation of the texts furnished by Holy Scripture. Its task can never be to try to get behind the witness of these texts. But it repeats in explanatory form what the witness as such declares, what prophets and apostles testify of the " mighty acts of God ". Now there is also another way of regarding this event, and this witness to the event. There is an untheological exegesis. There is the great undertaking of the *modern science of history*. By that I would understand the endeavour to peel off as far as possible, from reports of past events, all that is the contribution of the narrators and so expose what is " actually " the object of the reports (i.e. what is done and experienced by men). This object has to be worked out by the application of the categories of historical *relation* and historical *analogy*. The report under consideration is measured by them ; they are the criterion, or, rather the probability-test for the discrimination and appraisal of the reports. The report is accordingly classified as history or, on the other hand, as myth, saga or legend. If the report does *not* conform with the categories, the historian speaks of myth, saga, or legend. The modern science of history employs a reckoning of probability which rests on a conception of truth which is quite definitely limited. Its categories make no provision for the idea of a God Who acts in history and testifies to Himself in history. In spite of all that, there can be no fundamental obstacle to the application to the Bible also of this procedure of the modern science of history. The Bible is certainly, among other things, a human document. That there is no denying, and the consequences of it are by no means merely deplorable. Why should it not be possible for the scientific method of history to render its quite definite *services* to the investigation and exposition of the texts of Scripture? Theological exegesis itself is able to learn from it quite definite things. It is hard to see why this method should have to call a halt outside the Theological Faculty. Why should it not be *applied* in order to render its services to theological exegesis? Except that it must not raise the claim to be *the* method for true exegesis! It can be no more than a definite procedure which can be applied to the Bible among other methods, and which, precisely in its " atheistic " character, can perform the service of removing impurities. The Bible is a *human* document, having its place in the whole history of religion. The modern science of history makes it possible for us to understand this human document on its human side, and consequently to understand it as *witness* in a way that was not yet open to the Reformers.—And now at this point problems naturally crop up. Directing its inquiry always into the human occurrence as such, the method of the modern science of history cannot be identical with theological exegesis. If it is not to be recognised as human occurrence, then there is no positive statement to be made about it at all. Further, the mere interpretation of texts is not enough for it, but it must push on from the texts to what lies behind them. The theologian therefore has an attitude to, say, a chapter of Matthew's Gospel or even of John's different from that of the historian. To the

188

former the all-important thing is the *text* as such, while the latter, abstracting from the text, inquires " how it was ". Accordingly there are no clashes between theological exegesis and the historical science when historical science recognises the content of a text as *historical*. Things are different when the historian thinks it incumbent on him to speak of " saga " or " legend ". And yet I should have thought that this would have given *no* grounds for protest on the part of the theologian. The two conceptions obviously mean no more than that the reports are dealing with an event which as human event is problematical and which human thought, with its categories of relation and analogy, working on the basis of that limited conception of truth, finds it hard or impossible to explain. If only the theologians of the nineteenth century had not on their part succumbed to the historical way of thought, but had held fast to the wisdom of the Fathers, " It is written ! " there would have been none of this difficulty in the situation as between exegesis and historical science. Strictly speaking, the protest of the theologian can only begin where the historian speaks of " *myth* ". A report that is to be understood as " myth " has not its basis in any event, nor even in something " said " to have taken place. Here, on the contrary, is nothing but a human fantasy, a speculation about God and man. With the introduction of the idea of myth, theology sees its very *presupposition* attacked. There is nothing for it to do here but reject the historical method. In spite of this the dialogue between exegesis and historical science can go on : it is notorious that the most interesting conversations frequently take place when people are no longer talking to one another ! The theologian may then ask the historian whether the reason of his finding myths in the Bible may not be that he is himself an all-too mythical thinker, as indeed there has scarcely ever been thought so mythical as that of the nineteenth and twentieth centuries and so on.

We must not be surprised continually to meet texts in the Bible that are not able to hold out in face of the conception of truth held by historical science, but that the historian will be able to classify only as " saga " or " legend ". But just these texts draw our attention to the fact that, while the Bible is concerned with a *happening*, it is the happening of the mighty act of *God ! Qualiter ? totaliter aliter* than every other happening ! There is no more to be said ; and I shall take good care in dealing, for example, with the Virgin Birth, not to add one single word to what is there stated. There must be no question of explanation, of envisaging in the historical sense.

And now in this connection one of you has put to me concretely the specifically Dutch question, whether the serpent in Paradise " really " spoke ?—I would decidedly oppose characterising this incident as " myth ". No more can I, on the other hand, characterise it, in the sense of historical science, as " historical," for a speaking serpent —now, indeed, I am as little able to imagine that (apart from everything else !) as anyone. But I should like to ask the dear friends of the speaking serpent whether it would not be better to hold fast to the fact that this " is written " and to go on and interest themselves in *what* the serpent spoke ? To me they appear to be very important and momentous words that I should not like under any circumstances to miss from the Bible. The serpent's speech is indeed the invitation to man to face God with that question so significant for the very problem of theological exegesis : " Hath God said ? " Where this question is heard, there a man *must* have the idea of being as God, there the fruit *must* be eaten. There he stands reflecting over the Word of God, and to that Word he will then most *certainly* not be obedient. The attitude of standing over it critically, as also of standing over it apologetically, should be given up. The fact that we do not give it up proves very palpably that the serpent *has* really spoken, yes, indeed !

VI. The Government of the Church

In view of the questions you have put to me in this connection, I can only point with emphasis to the Word of Jesus, " *All* power is given unto Me in heaven and in earth ". He Who says that is the Lord both of the Church *and* of the world. But only as the Lord of the *Church* will it be possible for Jesus to be manifest to us ; as the Lord of the *world* He is hidden from us. We cannot get a knowledge of His government from the world's events, though we are certainly concerned there with none other power than His. This cannot mean under any circumstances that we are given two view-points, like the watchword which, I am told, once passed in Holland, 1. It is written, 2. It has happened ! Only in the Lord of Scripture and thereby of the Church can we seek and worship the Lord of history. And if we are going to be obedient to the Lord of the *world*, that can only be by our obeying the Lord of the *Church*. God's *voluntas revelata* and *voluntas arcana* cannot be differentiated from each other. Therefore there must be no intrusion here of any faith derived from history, any interpretation of history, any philosophy of history. In the midst of the world's events, in history, we must learn to listen to the *Word*, we must be obedient to *Scripture*, obedient to *Christ*.

But Jesus Christ rules His Church as the Risen One, as He Who, as the Victor over death, met His disciples through His Word and through His Spirit which He gave to them. *He* Who hears *you*, hears Me ! Christ rules His Church through Holy Scripture. " I am with you alway, even unto the end of the world ! " That means concretely, I am with you in this witness. *Scripture* rules the Church, so the Church cannot admit any kind of Papacy. To man there remains only the *ministry* of the Word of God ; he has no sovereignty there that might thrust itself into the place of Christ. The sovereignty is in the hands of Jesus Christ Himself, or with the witness to Him which it is the Church's task ever and again to cause to be proclaimed anew. All " Church-govern-mental " acts can therefore at bottom only be the act wherein *that* Church government is renewed which is entirely in the hands of Jesus Christ Himself.

VII. COMMUNIO SANCTORUM

(*a*) I have been directed to Article 27 of the *Confessio belgica,* in which the Church is described as *coetus omnium vere fidelium Christianorum.* The view is that it is better to hold fast to the *communio* of the *sancti,* since the certainty of faith might be undermined in interpreting it as *sancta.* But now it is actually the case that this formulation of Article 27 in the *Conf. belg.* is supplemented with a relative clause, *qui totam suam salutem in uno Jesu Christo expectant, sanguine ipsius abluti, et per Spiritum eius sanctificati atque obsignati.* Here in this clause we are directed to the great objective *sancta,* to the action of Jesus Christ. It is impossible to describe the *sancti* without this hint at the *sancta*. Heidelberg Catechism, Q. 55. In *Confessio Augustana* Article VII it is said, *congregatio sanctorum, in qua evangelium pure docetur et sacramenta recte administrantur*. The *vocatio interna* rests on a *vocatio externa*; it is to that that the *sancta* point. To be in the Church can only mean to be in *grace* and therefore in participation of those treasures entrusted to the Church. If we were to speak in isolation of *sancti* we should, in our interpretation of the conception of the Church, be approaching perilously near the congregational idea, and not stop till we landed at the idea of the religious association.

(*b*) In the same connection, strange to say, I was also asked the opposite question. It would only tolerate hearing of the *sancta* and, at that, the *sancta* understood as *sacramenta*. Certainly the *sacramenta* also belong to the *sancta*. But I should recommend care, and in no case should I interpret *sancta* exclusively as *sacramenta*. *Sancta* comprehend the divine act of revelation and of reconciliation and the existence, based on this act in the Holy Spirit, of the Church in time, in the world, in history—of the Church understood as totality of the signs, *signa*, that are displayed here: the assembly of the *fideles*, the sermon, the Sacraments, the Bible—all of which point to this divine act. It could be said, using the terms in this sense, that the Church is the *sacramental* place, i.e. the place of the *signa*. The place of the Church is bounded by the Sacraments; the way of the Christian is the way from Baptism to Holy Communion, just as the Church is on the way from memory to expectation. And to that extent the whole no doubt allows itself to be explained and seen under the conception of Sacrament also. But not for a moment must it be forgotten that it is the *coetus fidelium* which makes this place what it is. It is not something objective in itself : that would be a philosopheme. The Church is not only place, it is *ecclesia*. It is *congregatio sanctorum*, i.e. assembly of *men* who see these signs, who are called by them, for whom there exists, in face of these signs, the great possibility of *faith*. We cannot speak of the *vocatio externa* without also at the same time speaking of the *vocatio interna*. It is as little permissible to divorce the *sancta* from the *sancti* as the reverse. And so I should like to encourage the two last questioners to correct each other that both of them may then hit the mark.

(c) Finally, I was questioned about the scope of the *communio sanctorum*, and in particular as to the membership of the angels. If by *communio sanctorum* we understand the Church, then the question about the membership of the angels is to be answered in the negative. Church, understood in the sense of the Reformers, is an assembly of *men*. Even the conceptions *sancti* and *sancta* obviously refer to men who have sinned and who are now reconciled to God in Christ. To apply this statement to angels would be meaningless.

On the other hand, I can give an affirmative answer to the second question of the same questioner. To the *communio sanctorum* belongs not only the *ecclesia militans* but also the *ecclesia triumphans*, belongs therefore the communion of the blessed who have gone before us. Here, too, I should like to draw a line and issue a warning against exuberant fancies. What do we really know of the members of the Church who have gone before us, of the choir of Church Fathers, Church teachers and

Reformers and all the rest who have believed, loved and hoped before us ? We know them, as a matter of fact, only as members of the *militant* Church ; it is only after the flesh that we know even Martin Luther whose way from monk to Church Father was verily a way within the *ecclesia militans.* All that is included in the conception *triumphans* is accessible to us only in faith. The weakness of almost all Christian biographies is just that their authors do not hesitate to depict the " triumph " of the heroes, thus making it difficult for us to get a right view of the *ecclesia militans*, in order, in lieu of that, to weary us with fanciful pictures of another world which certainly is not the other world of God. We have to look for the Church under the *Cross.*

VIII. The Pluriformity of the Church

By pluriformity of the Church I understand the fact of the more or less sharply accentuated and partly harmless, partly perilous divisions in the Church.

When we confess our faith in the Church of Christ we confess our faith in the *one* Church, the *una sancta ecclesia.* This *una sancta* finds its expression in the fact that, in believing in the Church, we do not believe in an *idea* of the Church, but in the concrete Church to which we happen to belong, i.e. in which we are baptised. For us Reformed it is therefore the Reformed Church. As certainly as Church is *coetus fidelium*, just as certainly is it an actual visible assembly of men, just as certainly can it be the object of faith only where these men are.— The fact of the fragmentation of the *una sancta* belongs to the actual marks of the Church, and it is an indication that the Kingdom of God has in time only come near.

We must not take that to mean that it is possible for us to *trace* therein a *plan* of God and even perhaps to be delighted at this marvellous multiplicity and opulence. That is a profane point of view, applicable perhaps to " mankind," but not to the Church. When I see another faith, hear another doctrine, perceive another formation of the Church, all of which absolutely challenge me to a decision, how could I still be in the position to admire the manifoldness that to be sure is so clearly visible ? Where faith and confession are taken seriously, there is no room for " With one embrace I greet you, millions ". Were it a matter of human " opinions," that, of course, would be possible. But since it is a matter of division in the *Church*, we can recognise these divisions only with *horror* and can only *pray* for their removal. We verily believe in the *one* Church. We can see here nothing but an *affliction* of the Church, which we must believe will be *overcome*, though in truth the power to overcome it is not in our hands.

With regard to the division we have to distinguish between *other Churches* and *false Churches*. The other Churches we shall be able to recognise in their difference as " sister Churches ". The false Churches cannot be so described. An example of these other Churches, one that, as constituted, is not for us very readily approachable, one that we have a certain difficulty in understanding, is the *Lutheran* Church. Perhaps in listening to a Lutheran sermon I feel a slight uneasiness at not finding the sovereignty of God sufficiently acknowledged—a consequence of the Lutheran's inclination to allow a certain independent value to the creature—at finding the doctrine of sanctification curtailed, at finding his understanding of " office " unpleasing and untrustworthy, and so on.

But, in spite of these queries, it is not made impossible for me to recognise here the one Church, to have real fellowship in the faith with Lutherans or to take part in the Lutheran Communion service. A *union* between Lutherans and Reformed is not in principle impossible.

But there is that other side of the pluriformity of the Church, the possibility of the false Church. We can be confronted with Churches where there is no longer any question of recognising the one true Church, but in face of which we see ourselves forced to make a decision. For example, the Roman Catholic dogma of the infallibility of the Pope jeopardises the Sovereignty of Christ in a way that makes it impossible for me to recognise the Church where this dogma is in force. Equally pertinently I could name the doctrine of justification of the Council of Trent, which conceals the doctrine of free grace, or the sacramental doctrine of the Florentine Council, which implies a denial of the authority of the *Word* in the Church. —But even in regard to this state of affairs, it will be necessary to say : God's ways are different from our ways. He knows His own in places where we cannot imagine them. In the Roman Church also, Baptism is solemnised, and the Holy Communion, even if in a terribly distorted form, is administered ; in the Roman Catholic Church also the Bible is expounded, shaming us with the seriousness and the zeal with which it is done in many places. *In so far as* even there *evangelium pure docetur et sacramenta recte administrantur* we can and must certainly believe in *the* Church even within the *false* Church.

In this connection I was asked about the conception " Protestantism ". This word describes the *polemical* character of the true Church, but it does not exhaust the conception of the *evangelical* Church. It " protests " against man, who would fain set himself in the place of God, and against " justification by works," in regard to which it is well to reflect that as early as the sixteenth century this protest was directed not only against *Rome*, but also against the *fanatics* (*Schwärmer*). In the 400 years since the Reformation Protestantism has experienced a grave change ; rationalism and pietism tried to reintroduce man and his rights in opposition to God, and the Church largely succumbed to their efforts. Having itself become papist Church, it thereby lost in great measure the inner right to protest against Rome.—Let the Evangelical Church take pains to be *evangelical*, in order so to become anew really Protestant.

IX. Sermon and Sacrament

Question 66 of the Heidelberg Catechism runs, " What are the Sacraments ? The Sacraments are visible, holy signs and seals, appointed by God for this end, that by the use thereof they may *the more fully* declare and seal to us the promise of the Gospel, namely, that He grants us out of free grace the forgiveness of sins, and everlasting life for the sake of the one sacrifice of Christ accomplished on the Cross ".—The question put to me about the relationship of Sacrament and sermon I should like to answer first of all with a slight warning. Do not go to work here with the conceptions " objective " and " subjective," and do not imagine that you are compelled to set the objectivity of the Sacraments in opposition to the subjectivity of the sermon ! That is to make a very precarious assumption—one, I should say, that argues little faith—the assumption that the preacher " speaks subjectively ". The presupposition of the sermon, on the contrary, is just that the subjectivity of the preacher bows down under the objective word of the prophets and apostles and under the Word of God to which they bear witness. Certainly we have no guarantee that actually *that* is expressed, actually *that* is heard. And in view of the experiences of the last 200 years the temptation would seem to be very natural to take refuge from the all-too-subjective objectivity of the sermon in the " objectivity " of the Sacrament ! And yet this is an error. Not in the Sacrament is true objectivity contained, but in the Scriptures, in Christ. To seek it in the Sacrament would mean no more and no less than to deny the truth that the Reformation apprehended. Anyone failing to under-stand that the Roman Mass, so far as it rests on the doctrine of transubstantiation, is really, as the Heidelberg Catechism, Q. 80, says, " accursed idolatry," would do much better to become at once, completely and openly, a Roman Catholic. Here it can only be, Either—Or.

The other question was whether the special feature of the Sacrament did not consist in there being in it a " profoundest condescension of God ". I cannot, how-ever, find in this expression a peculiar characteristic of the Sacrament as contrasted with the sermon. Is it not profoundest condescension also that I, poor preacher, am to utter the Word of God ? If there is any sign of God's profound condescension, it is the presence of us theo-logians in the pulpit !—I should like to mark off the boundary-line differently, in this way. In the sermon a man speaks ; the sign is here the word of man. Even in the Sacrament there is speech, but the characteristic feature is what is done, the sign of immersion in water, of receiving food and nourishment. The Sacrament appears to me to go up to the sermon and to point out : There is not merely *speaking* here, but here something is done ! And what is done is just the event indicated in the Sacrament—the birth of the new man, his support and nourishment in the spiritual life. To the spoken word is added the action. In describing the essence of the Sacrament Calvin liked the idea of the *seal*. As the king is present in his seal and gives importance to the contents of the letter, so the Sacrament is conjoined with the sermon as sign of Christ present and acting.— With regard to the Sacrament the Evangelical Church has made a grave mistake. There is undoubtedly a connection between the neglect of the Sacrament and Protestantism's becoming Modernist. Certainly the sermon is the proper cultus-act, but it ought never to have been isolated in the way this happened in the Evangelical Church. As the seal is the reminder of the action of the King, and as such indispensable, so the Sacrament (observe, not the Sacrament in the Roman Catholic sense !) must come again into its own. It should be obligatory for the Holy Communion to be celebrated at *every* service, which is, as is well known, what Calvin strove for. To be complete an evangelical service should have to begin with Baptism, follow that up with the sermon and conclude with the Holy Communion. Then all these " liturgical movements " would be superfluous !

In pointing out the event-character of the Sacrament, I must not be understood as implying that the sermon as such is not also *event*. The two must not be separated. Baptism and Holy Communion are in their way proclamations of the *Word ;* so, on the contrary, the sermon is also something *done*. We must learn to understand anew this mutual relationship.

X. The Continuity of Faith

Two questions are to be discussed, the question of the continuity of the old and new man, and the question of the continuity of the single act of faith.

(a) How is the *continuity between the regenerated and the natural man* to be conceived ? I might answer with the counter-question, Must this continuity be *conceived ?* Is it necessary and is it possible to conceive to what extent I am in the flesh and in Christ, to what extent I am *iustus et peccator ?* Is it possible to conceive it ; is it *permissible* to conceive it ? Is there a third, neutral place, from which looking out we could survey our " Lord, I believe, help Thou mine unbelief " ? Would not any synthetic word imply that we were falsifying the nature of these two realities and taking the pith out of them ? Of the old and new man the New Testament is able to say no more than that the old man is *dead*, the new is *risen*. Here flesh stands in opposition to spirit, spirit to flesh. Here there is a battle waged, here a road is travelled, here a work is done. That is all that can be said about it. If standing between two possibilities I am to decide for one, I must make a turn. The unity of these two possibilities is in God, Who turns me away from the one and towards the other. Fundamentally it might however be said with regard to the continuity between the two that God's having *patience* with me is the basis of it, God's letting me still have time to make this turn. When I look at myself, all that remains for me to say is : How strange that I am still here and still the same old sixpence that I was yesterday, not one whit better. We all of us, looking at ourselves, can say nothing else. And then we open the Bible and read : " Let My *grace* be *sufficient* for thee!" To think that such wretches as we could have this said to us! In face of this, all that can be done is—each day anew—to praise and extol God. In face of this we can only be *ashamed* and at the same time listen to the *summons* of that Word, knowing that *death* is what we deserve and that we are actually allowed to *live*, reaching forth unto those things which are before. It is in this movement that we may exist, absolutely seriously and for that very reason not without humour also.—Only *faith* can have any perception of our victory, our progress. "All things work together for good to them that love God." In consequence of that there is each day anew comfort given and the journey renewed. But also each day anew in every fresh situation the sinful man in his totality will stand face to face with the grace of Christ in its totality. Particularly in the old Reformed Church the thought of progress in the Christian life played a rôle that was not entirely unambiguous. Actual progress will show itself concretely just in this: that we understand better and better that we are absolutely dependent on grace. As Luther said at the *end* of his life, "It is verily true; we are beggars!" That is the only sense in which we can speak of the victory of faith.

(*b*) With regard to the *continuity of the single act of faith* it must be pointed out that actually each act of faith represents a totality. In each act of faith I am completely put in question: This, thy brother, was *dead* and is alive again. Each act of faith is a *new* answer to a new question of God. But the act of faith is our adjustment to *Christ* Who came and Who comes again, Jesus Christ the same yesterday and to-day and for ever. Because Christ is its object, faith is confronted by what is immovable. That which from our point of view is an event, a here and now, is from God's point of view something eternal, abiding. This contradiction in the act of faith cannot and must not be resolved. Our life that takes place in the *communio sanctorum*—I am thinking of the *sancta*—the promise given us, the memory and expectation we have to cherish, all point us to that which abides. The consolation of the *eternal* God is the content of *temporal* faith. This difference is reflected in the difference between *faith* and *devoutness*. Devoutness we might describe as the readiness for that act of faith which at the moment is in prospect. Devoutness would say: memory and expectation. Though in itself meaningless (Religion and Christianity have in themselves no salvation value!), it has even so as promise (Sacrament!) a share also in the continuum, present in faith, of the divine consummation.